Preaching and Reading the Old Testament Lessons:

With an Eye to the New

Cycle A

Elizabeth Achtemeier

CSS Publishing Company, Inc., Lima, Ohio

Library of Congress Cataloging-in-Publication Data

Achtemeier, Elizabeth Rice, 1926-
    Preaching and reading the Old Testament lessons : with an eye to the new, Cycle B / Elizabeth Achtemeier.
    p. cm.
    ISBN 0-7880-1870-1 (alk. paper)
    1. Bible. O.T.—Homiletical use. I. Title.
BS1191.5 .A235   2001
251'.6—dc21   2001037905
                                                                      CIP

For more information about CSS Publishing Company resources, visit our website at www.csspub.com.

ISBN 0-7880-2321-7   PRINTED IN U.S.A.

*"The word of God
will stand
forever."*

Table Of Contents

Introduction

This volume contains 85 homiletical expositions of the Old Testament lessons (including the stated Lutheran options during the Pentecost season) in Cycle A of the Revised Common Lectionary. All of these were originally published by CSS Publishing Company in their magazine intended for pastors, *Emphasis*, beginning in the November/December 1998 issue (Volume 28, Number 4) and extending through the November/December 1999 issue (Volume 29, Number 4). Because the stated lectionary lessons change little from year to year, it was decided to assemble these expositions into one volume for the use of pastors, homiletical instructors, and interested lay people. The volume for Cycle B was published in 2002; the volume for Cycle C, in 2003.

The expositions contained here are not intended as substitutes for the minister's own sermon preparation nor are they complete sermons, although they are written in a homiletical style. Rather they are intended for the church and are brief presentations of the kerygmatic meaning of the stated texts in their historical contexts and in relation to the New Testament. They are intended to stimulate the development of truly biblical sermons, anchored in the biblical texts and related to our common life. But their messages also should be useful for private or group study of the stated texts and for homiletical instruction in the methods of explicating the Bible's message.

Much attention is given not only to the historical, but also to the canonical contexts of the various texts. I am very aware of the fact that the Old Testament is an unfinished book, with many of its motifs and theologies left incomplete and its divine promises left unfulfilled. Very often, therefore, the exposition moves into the New Testament and a discussion of the work of our Lord. In addition, there are frequent citations in parentheses of other Old and New Testament texts related to the passage under discussion. If the reader will consult such citations, the Bible's own interpretation of itself will be illumined, the reader's knowledge will be enlarged, and preachers will be furnished with a wealth of sermonic material related to the text for the day.

Unless noted, the biblical text used is the RSV (Revised Standard Version), with very limited reference to other translations. The New Revised Standard Version (NRSV) has not been used because it is my view, and the view of many other scholars, that while there are no objections to the generic language used in the NRSV, that version sometimes softens the meaning or alters the structures of the biblical texts found in the original Hebrew and Greek of the scriptures. Similarly, I do not employ the New International Version (NIV), which seems to be the favorite of conservatives in the church. After working very closely with the NIV and comparing it to the original Hebrew of the Old Testament, I found that it sometimes omits important words in its translation from the Hebrew or occasionally resorts almost to a paraphrase of the original text. (See my commentary, *Minor Prophets I, New International Biblical Commentary*, Hendrickson Publishers, 1996).

As I have studied these biblical texts and written these expositions I have continually been enlightened and fed by the Word of God. Sometimes that word has taken me in directions I never intended when I first sat down to write. The Word of God has more power than any interpreter of it can ever convey, and no expositions such as these can adequately mediate that saving power. There is no substitute for reading and studying and meditating and praying the biblical texts for ourselves. And there is no substitute for letting the texts themselves shape the sermon, the teaching, and the proclamation of the gospel. If this volume simply stimulates the study and aids in the announcement of the biblical word for our time, it will have been worth the effort involved in its writing.

— Elizabeth Achtemeier
Richmond, Virginia

First Sunday in Advent

Isaiah 2:1-5

We sometimes wonder what the world is coming to these days, and when we look at present conditions, we do not find very much that reassures us. Our nation is suffering a thorough-going breakdown of morality, with violence and wrong, selfishness and cynicism surrounding us on every side. Our world is full of poverty and hunger, wars and rumors of war, and whole populations subjected to tyranny and massacre. And try as we will to ameliorate conditions and to introduce some healing and good in society and world, any corrections we make seem like pitiful contributions compared to the force of evil in the world. Is that force finally just going to have the last word in human life and overwhelm us all?

If we believe that the course of nations and persons is determined solely by human endeavor, then we do not have many grounds for hope. Human sin has corrupted God's good creation and turned it into the scene that we see today. But if we believe, as the prophets believed, that God is the Lord who is finally in charge of the lives and course of all of us, then there is every reason to look to the future with confidence. Isaiah puts it very clearly in our Old Testament lesson for the morning.

"In the latter days," he proclaims, that is, in that indeterminate time in the future — in the fullness of God's purpose — when he brings in his kingdom on earth, even as it is in heaven, all nations and people will turn to the worship and guidance of the one Lord of history. That proclamation is very much like that statement of Paul's, that every knee will bow and every tongues confess that Jesus Christ is Lord, to the glory of God the Father (Philippians 2:10-11).

At that time, Mount Zion, where God dwells in the temple (cf. Psalm 76:2), will figuratively become the most important mountain in the world. Some read that as "the highest mountain," but it

11

is Zion's importance that will be elevated. We need not take that literally, but rather as a figure of God's decisive consequence for human history.

To that mountain, to God, all nations and peoples will flow in one great pilgrimage. In other words, Isaiah is picturing the world-wide conversion of all peoples to the God of the Bible. We find the same announcement in Psalm 102:21-22; Jeremiah 3:17; Zephaniah 3:9-10; and Zechariah 8:20-22; this is a frequent announcement in the Old Testament. Moreover, not only will persons themselves turn to God, but they will also urge their friends and companions to join them in their conversion, symbolized by their trek to Zion (v. 3).

The reason why all will travel to Mount Zion is given in the second half of verse 3. They turn to God in order to receive his instruction in how to behave. To learn God's "ways" and to "walk in his paths" means to be taught by God, to have him explain how to conduct oneself, to be shown the way in which to walk. So "torah" in this verse has its basic meaning of "teaching." It concerns not just the law, but the whole of God's will about how to live one's life. And the nations, in our text, have realized that true wisdom about how to think and believe and act comes not from human beings, but from God alone. We need the revelation of God's will in order to live properly — that will which is revealed by the Lord God alone. (Again, one is reminded of Paul's words in 1 Corinthians 2:6-13.)

Not only does God teach, according to our passage, but he also acts as a judge and arbiter between nations (cf. Psalm 76:9; 96:13; 98:9), to settle the inevitable disputes that arise among peoples, all of whom are so different from one another because of their various backgrounds and languages, geography and customs. Both of the terms, "judge" and "decide" in verse 4, are legal terms. And God alone is the only one who can render righteous and just and equitable decisions. He is not subject to human prejudices and self-seeking, not influenced "by what his eyes see or what his ears hear" (Isaiah 11:3). Above all, he restores to the poor and oppressed their rightful place in society (Isaiah 11:4).

So just and fair are God's decisions among peoples, moreover, that they need not try to win their own advantage through the use of power, and they need not try to foist their will on others. Rather, they gladly accept God's judicial decisions and renounce all attempts to win their own way by the use of arms. They beat their swords into plowshares and their spears into pruning hooks (v. 4). Those weapons that had been instruments of destruction and death are transformed into tools of production and life-giving sustenance. God's teachings and his decisions bring forth not death to human beings, but the goodness and abundance of life.

Verses 2-4 of our text are paralleled in the prophecy of Micah 4:1-3, and both Micah and Isaiah are drawing on a common tradition about the future. But they end their proclamations differently. Here in verse 5 of the Isaiah passage, Judah of the eighth century B.C. is issued a call to faith in their sovereign God, who will finally bring to earth his just and right and loving order. "Walk in the light of the Lord," Judah is admonished. That is, walk by the Word of God, which in the scriptures is always the source of true light (cf. John 1:4).

In Micah 4:4-5, however, the promise of God's good kingdom is given poignant illustration in verse 4 by the picture of every one sitting under his own vine and fig tree, without any fear. And in verse 5, Judah speaks its affirmation of faith, stating that other peoples may walk according to the will of their gods, but that Israel will walk by the will of the one true God alone.

When we read and hear these promises from the prophets, we are given the sure basis of Christian hope, namely, that our lives and our history are finally not in our own hands, but in the loving hand of the God and Father of our Lord Jesus Christ. He is at work in human history, slowly, continually, to restore the goodness to his creation that he intended it to have in the beginning. And these promises from the prophets of the Old Testament find their confirmation in the words and finally the death and resurrection of our Lord. "I, when I am lifted up from the earth," Jesus promises, "will draw all people to myself" (John 12:32). Jesus replaces the temple of Zion, in the New Testament (John 2:19-21), and it is to him that all peoples will flow for instruction, for judgment, and for salvation. That is the Word of the Lord.

Second Sunday in Advent

Isaiah 11:1-10

This passage is part of the larger section of Isaiah 10:5—11:16, that portrays the defeat of Assyria, the gathering of the remnant of Israel that was deported to Assyria in 721 B.C., and the defeat of Israel's enemies. Specifically, it deals with the future ideal time, when Israel's messianic king will rule in a blessed kingdom of peace.

Our word for messiah comes from the Hebrew *masiah*, which means "anointed," and it refers to the anointed davidic king. During the reign of David in the tenth century B.C., God promised that there would never be lacking a davidic heir to sit upon the throne (2 Samuel 7:13, 16). To realize the importance of that, we must understand that Israel's life was bound up completely with its davidic ruler, whose righteousness before God insured that the people were also counted righteous in God's eyes — the king was the corporate representative of the people. Israel therefore looked for that perfect davidic ruler to come, and of every occupant of the throne, the people inquired, "Are you the one who is to come, or should we look for another?" God's promise in this passage, therefore, is that such a messiah will indeed come and make his people righteous in the sight of God.

There is a certain disgust with the line of Israel's davidic rulers mirrored in verse 1. None of them has been the fulfillment of Israel's expectation of a saving messiah. None has measured up. But the promise here in our text is that such a messiah will come, and a description of his character is given in detail.

Most importantly, the coming messiah will be given the Spirit of the Lord that will rest or remain with him permanently (v. 2). Usually in the scriptures, the Spirit is given only temporarily in order that a task may be done, but the messiah will have the Spirit as a permanent endowment, and it is that Spirit that furnishes him with all of his qualities. Significantly, therefore, our Lord receives the Spirit of God at his baptism, and John 1:32 states that the Spirit descends upon Jesus and *remains* with him. We can therefore say that the picture of the coming davidic messiah that we have in this passage is also the picture of our Lord Jesus Christ, whose birthday we remember in this Advent season and whose second coming we look forward to.

From the Spirit, states our text, the messiah will receive a sixfold gift (v. 2). He will be given the Spirit of wisdom and understanding, so he will know the right thing to do. But he will also be given the Spirit of counsel and might, so that he has the power to put his wisdom into effect. The wisdom of human beings is distorted by sin, and though we think we can proceed according to our own plans, apart from the Word and Spirit of God, our autonomous reason always leads us into disaster (cf. Isaiah 5:21; 29:14), a fact vividly illustrated in the morning headlines. Such is not the case with the messiah, however. He thinks and acts by the wisdom and power of God. As Jesus says, "The Son does nothing of his own accord, but only what he sees the Father doing" (John 5:19).

The messiah is also given the Spirit of knowledge and of the fear of the Lord. In the scriptures, knowledge of God is intimate, inmost knowledge of God's nature and will and actions. To know God is to live in intimate daily communion with him, while to fear God is to reverence him. Thus, God's messiah will live in the company of God in true worship and service.

Verse 3 tells us, moreover, that the messiah will delight in his obedience and worship of God. He will have joy in his life with God, that joy that Jesus and every true disciple knows. In contrast to those who think that obedience to God is a burden and worship a bore, here is the testimony that constant fellowship with God is delightful, because our God is indeed an enjoyable God. He is many other things, but he is also enjoyable.

The messiah comes to set our sinful world in order and to establish God's rule over all the earth. Thus, in this Advent season we not only look backward to the birth of Jesus, but we look forward to his coming again. And we are told in our text that he comes first of all to restore the helpless and meek of this earth to their proper place in society (v. 4). The messiah will not be swayed by earthly standards and judgment, not by outward evidences (cf. John 2:25; 7:24). Rather, he will judge in righteousness and equity, making that straight in society that has been crooked, restoring rights to the oppressed, and safety and security to the weak (cf. Isaiah 10:1-2; 32:1; Psalm 72:12-14), while at the same time condemning the wicked to death. Surely that is a cautionary warning to all of us who await the coming of our Lord.

When our messiah comes, however, the right that he restores to society will find its counterpoint in the natural world, where every kind of violence will be eliminated (vv. 6-8). Throughout the Bible, human sin is said to ruin the natural world (Genesis 3:17-18; 9:2; Jeremiah 12:4; Romans 8:19-23). But the messiah will establish peace in the animal kingdom, and peace between the wild beasts and human beings. The serpent of our sin, referred to in verse 8, will become a harmless plaything for children, and the peaceable kingdom will be one in which no one will ever again hurt or destroy (v. 9). The whole earth will obey and reverence God, and the Lord's universal kingdom will be established throughout the world. God's messiah comes to save all on this earth (cf. Isaiah 45:6; 52:10; 66:23).

Verse 10 is a later addition to our original text, and the "root of Jesse" here no longer stands for the origin of the messianic king, as in verse 1, but rather refers to the messianic king himself, who will be an ensign, that is, a standard, a signal, lifted up for all to see and to which all shall come, a note reminiscent of John 12:32. Verse 10 has been added as a transition to give the passage a universal note, but that is already found in the preceding verses. Verses 10-11 form a transition to verses 12-16.

What we finally have in our text, therefore, is a description of the One who was born at Bethlehem and of the same One who will come again to judge the earth and to establish God's kingdom. The passage is a vivid description of the character of our messiah, a revelation of the nature of the Lord whom we worship and serve.

Third Sunday in Advent

Isaiah 35:1-10

This passage has many affinities with the prophecies of Second Isaiah (Isaiah 40-55), and it has often been attributed to him. But there are differences. In Isaiah 40:3, the "way" is for the Lord, here it is for the redeemed and ransomed (vv. 9-10). In Isaiah 51:11, the reference is to the return from Babylonian exile. Here in verse 10, that context is missing, and those who are returning to Zion are the members of Israel dispersed throughout the ancient Near East. Thus, this text is probably from a time after Second Isaiah and sometime after 538 B.C. The problem that faces the preacher, however, is how to make this passage relevant for a modern congregation.

If we note the repetitions of words in the passage, it becomes clear that we have two strong figurative contrasts. First, there is emphasis on the dryness and heat of the desert (vv. 1, 6) which is a place of burning sand, thirsty ground, and the haunt of jackals (v. 7). That is contrasted with life-giving waters, streams (v. 6), a swamp, reeds and rushes (v. 7), and crocuses that grow abundantly in swampy land (v. 1). But as in Second Isaiah, the desert and wilderness are figures for life without God — its dryness, its thirst for something, its death. Contrarily, the references to water and the abundant life that it gives are figures for the life with God — its satisfaction of thirst and hunger, its vitality, its wholeness and permanence.

Other biblical passages immediately spring to mind in such a connection — the fact that those who follow the will of God are like trees planted by streams of water, that never wither and that bring their forth fruit in due season (Psalm 1:3); or the fact that Christ, the fountain of living water (John 7:38), can keep us from ever thirsting again (John 4:13). Thus, the preacher can contrast the old life without God, that so many in any congregation still know, with the fullness of life given by fellowship with God.

Alongside that, there is in our text a strong contrast set forth between the fear, sorrow, and sighing (vv. 4, 10) known to the old life, and the joy, gladness, and singing that are given in the new life with God (vv. 1, 2, 6, 10). And that goes along with the first contrast given above. Thus, the congregation, still immersed in the ways of B.C., can be given a picture of the life they may have in Jesus Christ, in A.D. But their question is: Will that life come to them?

The prophet announces in verses 3-4 that it will indeed come, that God is on the way, to avenge those who have done wrong and to save those who trust his coming. Indeed, the faithful will see the glory of the Lord (v. 2) — that is, God's presence on earth, which is the meaning of "glory" here. But is that not the message that we are given at Christmastime, that the glory of the Lord has shown in the heavens (Luke 2:9) and that in the babe of Bethlehem, we have in fact seen his glory, glory as of the only Son of the Father, full of grace and truth (John 1:14)? God has in truth come to us in his Son.

So those who are fearful, can take courage, and those who are weak can be strong (v. 4), for God has come to turn their desert of death into the eternal and watered abundance of life. In short, God has come to establish his kingdom of life on earth, even as it is in heaven.

That kingdom began in the birth of our Savior at Bethlehem. The Isaiah traditions repeatedly announce that when the kingdom comes, the blind and deaf, the lame and dumb will be restored to wholeness (vv. 5-6; cf. Isaiah 29:18-20; 32:3-4; 33:24; 42:7, 16). Thus when John the Baptist inquires who Jesus is, in our gospel lesson, he learns that the Son of God has indeed fulfilled that ancient prophecy (Matthew 11:2-11). The new life of the Kingdom of God has begun to break into our lives in the person of Jesus Christ! And the New Testament tells us that if we trust our Lord, we can begin to participate in the vitality and powers of that new age that he brings, leaving behind us the wilderness of death and the thirst of sin. We can begin now to inherit the goodness of the new age of the kingdom.

Our text not only applies to our lives now, however. It also holds out before us the picture of a glorious future. Intended originally for the people of Israel, dispersed throughout the Mediterranean world, this pronouncement by Isaiah pictures the time when the covenant people are gathered once again to the temple on Zion in Jerusalem to praise their Lord in joy and gladness (v. 10). God will prepare the way for them, announces the prophet, a "Holy Way," which means a way set apart for God's purpose. No one who has violated God's commandments (the "unclean") will walk the way, no wicked ("fools," as in Wisdom literature) will be found on it, and no natural enemies will prevent the return of the faithful. God will "redeem" or "ransom" his own from their captivity and dispersion among the nations, that is, he will buy them back. And faithful Israel will be free to return to her God and to his praise and worship.

Have we too not been "redeemed" by our God, bought back by the death and resurrection of his Son, and set free from our captivity to sin and death? And have we too not been given a "Holy Way" to return to the worship and praise of our God? But the "way" for us is Jesus Christ, who is the way, the truth, and the life, and through him, we all may return to fellowship with the Father. Indeed, Jesus Christ is now our incarnate temple, our place of worship (John 3:19-20; 4:21), and our return to him is our return to Zion.

But the picture is, you see, also a picture of the future, when not only we, but all the faithful throughout the world gather to Jesus Christ, and every knee bows and every tongue confesses that he is Lord, to the glory of God the Father (cf. Isaiah 45:23; Philippians 2:10-11). Then God's kingdom will have come on earth, and God will be all in all.

So strengthen your weak hands and make firm your feeble knees. Be strong and fear not! This day by trust in Jesus Christ, our Lord, who has come to us at Bethlehem, you may leave behind you the dust and dryness and death of your old life, and you may inherit the beginning of the watered, abundant life of God's new age, looking forward in joy and gladness to the future, when God's good kingdom will be established over all the earth.

Fourth Sunday in Advent

Isaiah 7:10-16

"O that thou wouldst rend the heavens and come down" (Isaiah 64:1). When we contemplate the evil and violence in our world, that is often our plea — for God to come down and to set things right. We need the power of God that can put down tyrants, the love of God that can replace hatred with mercy, the forgiveness of God that can wipe out all the guilty past and restore our hearts and the hearts of all human beings to peace and goodness. And the message at this Christmastime is that God has answered our plea; he has sent us a Savior to cleanse and restore his creation to goodness.

But what are we given for a Savior? A baby! The tiny infant of a lowly peasant woman and her carpenter husband, born in a stable and laid in a feed trough for cattle. A baby! Helpless, dependent, unable to speak or walk or feed himself. Is this the mighty Savior of the world? Is this the one whom God sends as the answer to our plea for rescue?

That also could have been the question that King Ahaz of Judah asked in our Old Testament text for the morning. For Ahaz is threatened by the armies of northern Israel and of Syria. The time is 734 B.C. in our text, during what is known as the Syro-Ephraimitic war. A century earlier, the small states along the Eastern coast of the Mediterranean had banned together and turned back the threatening armies of the Assyrian Empire. But now Assyria is threatening again, and Syria and Ephraim (northern Israel) want to form that alliance once more, with Judah as a partner in it. King Ahaz of Judah, however, wants no part of such an attempt, and he refuses to join his neighbors. As a result, Pekah of Israel and Rezin of Syria assemble their armies to march against Judah, to depose Ahaz, and to put a puppet on the Judean throne who will join their cause.

The word that is given to Ahaz by the prophet Isaiah is that if Ahaz will trust in the Lord, the Lord will preserve Ahaz' davidic kingdom and destroy the rulers of Israel and Syria. But what Ahaz needs is to believe that promise. However, proclaims Isaiah, "If you will not believe, you shall not be established" (Isaiah 7:9). Indeed, to prove to Ahaz that God will protect Judah, Isaiah offers a "sign" to Ahaz, and Ahaz can choose whatever sign he wishes (vv. 10-11).

Ahaz, who has already summoned Assyria to his aid, piously and hypocritically replies, "I will not put the Lord to the test" (cf. Deuteronomy 6:16). And that, says Isaiah, wearies the Lord God (v. 13), who cannot stomach such hypocrisy — piety apart from our heart's devotion is pain and weariness to the Lord (cf. Isaiah 1:14).

Nevertheless, continues Isaiah, God will give Ahaz a sign. A young woman of marriageable age will conceive and bear a son and call his name Immanuel (v. 14). As we know from our gospel lesson, the New Testament understood that as a prediction of the birth of Jesus Christ, reading "young woman" (*'almah* in the Hebrew) as "virgin" (*parthenos*) from the Septuagint. Originally, of course, the reference was not to a virgin or to Jesus. Rather the young woman was simply the wife of the prophet or, more probably, the wife of the king himself. And "Immanuel" was very likely a name that lots of women gave to their infants. But that common occurrence was to be the "sign" to Ahaz that God would keep his promise to him to defend him. God had much earlier promised that there would never be lacking a davidic heir to sit upon the throne (2 Samuel 7). You can trust that promise, Isaiah was assuring Ahaz. One thing, however, was required of that davidic king — faith. "If you will not believe, you shall not be established."

But, continues our text, because Ahaz has not believed and instead has summoned Assyria's armies to his aid, before the child Immanuel is able to have adult discernment between good and evil, Syria and Ephraim will be defeated, but Judah too will be devastated by Assyria, and the only food available will be not agricultural products, but curds from the herds and wild honey from the forests (vv. 15-16).

Certainly the prophecy by Isaiah proved true. In 721 B.C., the Assyrian Empire under Sargon II defeated Syria and northern Israel, and the inhabitants of the northern kingdom were taken into

24

exile and disappeared from history, never to be heard from again. Under King Ahaz and then King Hezekiah, Judah became a faithful vassal of Assyria until 701 B.C., when Hezekiah, against the advice of Isaiah, entered into an alliance with Philistia and revolted against Assyria, counting on the help of Egypt. Assyria under the rule of Sennacherib, therefore attacked Judah. Forty-six of her cities were crushed, and her complete destruction was prevented only by the payment of a heavy tribute. Judah did not believe in the Lord. Therefore she was not established, and she remained a vassal under the Assyrian yoke through most of the following seventh century B.C.

Ahaz was given a sign, a sign of a baby named Immanuel. And we too are given the same sign in the birth of Jesus at Bethlehem. "This shall be a *sign* for you," proclaimed the angel of the Lord in Luke's Christmas story. "You will find a babe wrapped in swaddling cloths and lying in a manger." And Joseph in Matthew's account is told by an angel in a dream to name that child Emmanuel (Matthew 1:23-24). Thus, Jesus Christ comes to us, not as a helpless infant, powerless to save, but as the mighty sign and Son of the God who will establish and save our lives if we trust in him. "If you do believe, you shall be established."

The Lord, you see, chooses strange ways to reassure us of his salvation, not by rending the heavens and coming down in some cataclysmic display of power, not by overwhelming us with terrifying visions, but by sending a prophet to speak words — words that are then fulfilled in the birth of a tiny child. And in that child lies our deliverance from evil, our forgiveness for sin, our death's defeat, and our sure hope of eternal life. If we believe that, we shall indeed be saved.

Christmas Eve Day

Isaiah 9:2-7

Our Christmas celebrations are associated with light. In our gospel lesson from Luke, there is the glory of the Lord shining on the shepherds, or in Matthew, the light of the star guides the Wise Men. We have the light of our Advent candles and lights on our Christmas trees. The outside of our houses or our city decorations sometimes are festooned with lights. Everywhere we employ special lights to celebrate the birth of Jesus Christ.

And that is fitting for our Old Testament text, because from it we hear that those of us who have walked in darkness — those of us who have known the gloom and the "deep darkness" of our sinful and suffering world — are delivered by Christ into a world of light, which is a symbol throughout the Bible for God's deliverance.

Originally, this text had nothing to do with Christmas and Christ, however. As we can see in verse 1, Isaiah composed it as a comforting proclamation for the inhabitants of northern Israel, in which the districts of Naphtali and Zebulon were included. Those Galilean territories had been conquered by the Assyrian ruler, Tiglath-pileser I in 733-732 B.C. and incorporated into the Assyrian Empire. They had been subjected to the "yoke" of slavery to Assyria. But when Hezekiah (727-698 B.C.) ascended the throne of Judah, Isaiah prophesied that the Lord would free the Galilean territories from their subjection to Assyria, reunite them with the southern kingdom, and bring in an everlasting realm of freedom and peace. Thus, this poem was probably composed for the coronation ceremony of Hezekiah.

The passage divides into three parts. Verses 2-3 tell of joy that has been given to the Israelites by God, a joy comparable to that found in the celebrations of an abundant harvest or military victory. (Most scholars emend verse 3a to read, "Thou hast brought them abundant joy" to preserve the parallelism.) But the reason for the joy is not immediately given. That is spelled out in three following sentences that begin with the important little Hebrew word *ki*, "for."

First, in verse 4, the people are joyful because they have been freed from their Assyrian conquerors. The oppression of Assyria's "yoke," like a yoke worn by a beast of burden, has been removed; the "staff" and "rod" with which slaves were beaten have been broken, and God has won a victory over Assyria comparable to that of Gideon's complete and lasting victory over the Midianites (Judges chs. 6-8).

Second, in verse 5, all the garments and accouterments of war have been burned up after God's victory, and cannot be used again. A universal peace is being prepared.

But third and climactically, in verse 6, a new ruler has ascended the throne of Judah. Isaiah frequently employs names to encapsule his message (cf. 8:1-3), and that is true here too. The new ruler is called "Wonderful Counselor." That is, unlike those kings who have followed bad advice, this king will share in the wisdom given by God (cf. 11:2) and will be able to put his plans into effect — in the scriptures, to know is also to be able to do.

The king will have the name "Mighty God," which is sometimes used of military heroes, but here it signifies the ruler's power for peaceful rule and his godlike character. He will have the name "Everlasting Father," which refers not to his continued existence, but to his endless care for his people. And the king will be a "Prince of Peace," sovereign over a universal realm of *shalom*, which signifies not only cessation from war but also fullness of life.

Then the announcement reaches its climax. This ruler will be a davidic king, whose rule or dynasty will never end. But his reign will be established, not by force and conquest, but by the moral qualities of justice and righteousness (cf. 11:3-5). That is, his rule will exhibit God's order for society and his fulfillment of God's will. And all of this will be given by God's actions, whose zeal for his purpose will establish it.

Isaiah is therefore announcing to the northern Israelites that Hezekiah's reign will not only bring the defeat of the Assyrian

Empire and Israel's freedom, but will also usher in a realm of universal *shalom*.

Sadly, Isaiah's hopes for Israel were disappointed. The inhabitants of the north were totally overrun by the Assyrians in 722-721 B.C. They were deported into Assyrian exile, their territories were turned over to foreigners, and they were lost forever to history. Similarly, Hezekiah himself remained a vassal to Assyria until his revolt in 701 B.C. But Judah's attempts at freedom were crushed, she lost much of her territory, and Hezekiah was made a virtual prisoner in Jerusalem, to be followed on the throne by his son Manasseh, who simply acceded to Assyrian demands and filled Judah's society with idolatry, syncretism, and corruption.

Was Isaiah's prophecy then false and were his hopes for a davidic Messiah then in vain? If that were the case, we would not have this text preserved in the Old Testament. These words were words of the Lord given to the prophet, and God always keeps his Word. This promise of a coming davidic ruler, who would match Isaiah's wondrous description of him, was preserved in Israel and kept for the future, because Israel knew and expected that a Messiah like this would come. But he would come in God's good time — not when human beings wished him to come, but when God so willed. Not we ourselves, but God is the Lord of our lives and history, and he works his own ways.

So it is, in the fullness of God's time, that we celebrate the birth of this davidic ruler, this Messiah, that God promised through Isaiah long ago. And this Messiah, Jesus Christ, is indeed the One who rules in the wisdom and might of God, who cares for us like a Father forever, and who will establish his reign of peace throughout the earth by his justice and righteousness.

Isaiah says that brings the light of God's deliverance to all of us — to us who sometimes think that we dwell and walk in nothing but darkness. Will you therefore trust that — that Christ will give light to your life if you but open your heart to his rule and let him direct your paths? If you will — if you will — then you too can have great joy and celebration at this Christmastime.

Christmas Day

Isaiah 52:7-10

"My way is hid from the Lord, and my right is disregarded by my God" (Isaiah 40:27). Thus did captive Israel mourn in Babylonian exile in the latter half of the sixth century B.C. But such mourning is not confined to any time period. There are a lot of people who, in this sacred season, would secretly say, "My way is hid from the Lord" — persons who are alone or despairing or suffering, who feel that God is nowhere near them — and Christmas can even exacerbate the feeling.

But Second Isaiah (Isaiah 40-55) announced good news to those despairing exiles, the good news that we find in our text for the day. Lift up your voice and sing for joy, he told his captive people, for God has not forgotten you; he is coming to redeem you, to buy you back, out of your subjugation (v. 9). Do you not see him coming? Behold! There! The Lord God comes in might and mercy, to "feed his flock like a shepherd" and to "gather the lambs in his arms" (Isaiah 40:11). He will save you in the sight of all of the nations (52:10) and lead you back to your own country. And so our text is followed by the command, "Depart, depart, go out thence ... for the Lord will go before you, and the God of Israel will be your rear guard" (vv. 11-12).

That is the message that is given us too on this Christmas Day — that God has not forgotten us and that we need not despair. Rather, the God of might and mercy has taken human flesh in the incarnation of his Son, and now he comes to each one of us to redeem us from our captivity to whatever suffering or sin we know, and to lead us back to return to life and joy and singing.

We find in our Old Testament passage the first use of the word "gospel," "good news," announced by an evangel, a messenger of good news (v. 7), and Second Isaiah borrows an ancient custom to set forth that joyous message.

31

When a new king was crowned in Israel and ascended to his throne, messengers were sent throughout the land to announce the beginning of his reign. "So and so reigns," they would proclaim, and that was always a cause for fresh hope and gladness, because it meant that a new era had begun and that perhaps life in the nation would be better than it had been in the past. Second Isaiah could therefore proclaim, "How beautiful upon the mountains are the feet" of those messengers who bring the good news (v. 7).

But the prophet put a new twist on that traditional custom. He does not announce that some human king has ascended to the throne. Rather he says, "Your God reigns!" The Lord God is sovereign. He rules over all of human life. That is indeed the gospel good news, and that is in truth the joyful message of this Christmas Day. In the birth of his Son at Bethlehem, God reigns, God is king over life, his is the kingdom and the power and the glory.

For the Israelites in Babylonian captivity, that meant that the mighty rulers of the Babylonian Empire were no longer in charge of their lives. Rather there was a greater One, a Ruler incomparable in power, for whom the nations were like a drop in the bucket (Isaiah 40:15), One who could bring princes to nought, and make the rulers of the earth as nothing (40:23), and so One who could free the exiles from the grasp of a foreign nation. The prophecy proved true, of course. Babylonia fell to Cyrus of Persia in 539 B.C., and Cyrus became the Lord's instrument to release the Israelites to return to Palestine (cf. Isaiah 45:1, 13).

Given the power of that merciful God, do you not know that he reigns in our lives and in your individual life also? He still rules over the world of nations. We sometimes think that our futures are determined solely by the powers of this world — by the politicians, the military, the multinational corporations — and we carry around the secret fear that they can at any time decree death for us and our world. But no. "Your God reigns," and the course of history is in his hand, and he is still at work, using rulers, shaping events, disposing of tyrants to move history along toward the goal of his kingdom.

And that Ruler of the world, that Sovereign over the nations, is the One who is incarnated for us in the birth of his Son at Bethlehem.

King Herod could not dispose of him after he was born, could he? And the Roman Empire could not kill him forever on a cross. Nor have any of his enemies ever been able to erase his name or saving power from history. His light shines in the darkness, and the darkness has not overcome it (John 1:5), because he is the Lord, and our God reigns in him.

Our God, yours and mine, also reigns over each of our lives. I suppose each of us carries around in our hearts the memory of a sinful past — of wrong we committed, of weakness or failure, of some terribly human evil. And the burden of our trespass against God or neighbor sometimes hovers over us like a menacing shadow. But do you think that the Lord who commands the nations and brings forth the stars every night can be helpless in the face of our sin? That he is powerless to erase the evil in our hearts and lives? No. "Comfort, comfort my people," says our sovereign God, for our "iniquity is pardoned" (Isaiah 40:1) through the Son of God, Jesus Christ. And his power can wipe out our past and give us a totally new beginning, transforming us into new creatures by the work of his Spirit in us. Your God reigns in your life, good Christians, and he comes to you at this Christmastime.

As for our suffering, our pain, our sorrow, that Shepherd who feeds his flock and gathers the lambs in his arms — that good Shepherd who carries us in his bosom and gently leads those that are with young (Isaiah 40:11) — rules over each one of our days in tenderness and mercy and comfort. He never deserts us in our tribulation, but says to us, "Fear not ... When you pass through the waters I will be with you; and through the rivers, they shall not overwhelm you; when you walk through fire you shall not be burned, and the flame shall not consume you. For I am the Lord your God ... Your Savior" (Isaiah 43:1-3). And so he not only abides with us and strengthens us, but he also defeats the power of the death that we and our loved ones face, and we now know that beyond the grave, there is his joyful life everlasting.

Your God reigns — over the world, over sin, over suffering, over death. Yes, that is indeed good news. That is gospel. And that is true because our Lord Jesus Christ has been born at Bethlehem.

First Sunday after Christmas

Isaiah 63:7-9

By specifying this text on the first Sunday after Christmas —
that day so often called "low Sunday," when the congregation is
small and everyone is rather exhausted from the Christmas celebration — the framers of the lectionary have intended these verses
to be simply a praise of the love and redemption that God has manifested in the birth of our Savior at Bethlehem, a sort of "marking
time," before we proceed with the church year.

Yet, the dark tones that we find in the gospel lesson prompt us
to see deeper meanings here, and that becomes evident when we
consider the context of this text. These verses form the first stanza
of the communal lament, that is found in 63:7—64:12 and that is
uttered by the Levitical-prophetic party in post-exilic Judah. The
standard form of such laments includes: 1) a recounting of God's
saving deeds in the past, as in verses 7-14; 2) a detailing of the
community's present desperate situation, in verses 63:15-19; and
3) a petition for help, verses 64:1-12. Thus the praise in our text,
verses 7-9, is uttered by those who must also confess that they
have been in their sins a long time, that they all have become like
one who is unclean, and that all their righteous deeds are like a
polluted garment, 64:5-6. That sets the context of our text.

That also sets the connection of our text with the congregation
— with us — however, for we who have received God's gift of the
Christ child are also those who have rebelled against him and
grieved his Holy Spirit (63:10). And all of us, who have celebrated
Christmas, are those who have seldom called upon the name of the
Lord and bestirred ourselves to take hold of him (64:7). What does
that say about the actions of God that are described in our text for
the morning?

First of all, God's coming to us in the birth of Jesus has been
totally undeserved on our part. Do any one of us deserve the

35

redemption that God has begun in the birth of his Son? Have we earned God's love for us? Obviously not. Rather, we have deserved God's judgment upon us for our neglect of his company and our violation of his commands given us in the scriptures. Our just deserts would be God's abandonment of us altogether.

And yet, God has clung to his covenant relationship with us. He has shown us "steadfast love," which means he has always been faithful to his covenant, as he was also faithful to his covenant with Israel. When the Lord delivered the Israelites from slavery in Egypt and entered into covenant with them at Mount Sinai, he promised them that he would be their God and they would be his special people, a nation set apart for his purpose (that is, a "holy nation") to be his "kingdom of priests," mediating the knowledge of him to the rest of the world (Exodus 19:4-6). And God has made the same promise to us (1 Peter 2:9-10).

Then through all the centuries of Israel's sin against him, God kept that promise, never deserting his people, but constantly forgiving and trying to instruct them and weeping over their evil deeds. And so too God in Jesus Christ has never deserted us, but has steadfastly clung to the covenant he makes with us every time we celebrate the Lord's Supper.

Israel became God's adopted children when he delivered them out of slavery (Isaiah 63:8; Exodus 4:22-23; Hosea 11:1; Jeremiah 30:20), and God became their Father, loving them with the love surpassing that of all earthly fathers (Isaiah 64:8; Jeremiah 3:19; 31:9). And so too when we were baptized, we were adopted as God's children, given his Spirit that allows us to call him "Abba! Father!" (Galatians 6:6-7), and to pray with confidence to "Our Father, who art in heaven...."

The steadfast covenant love that God gave to Israel and that he still gives to us is therefore a love of the most intimate care and concern. There is nothing legalistic about God's relation to us, no cut and dried demand that we follow every jot and tittle of his commandments, no wrathful punishment when we do not measure up and fail. No. God's steadfast love is the love of a Father who will not desert his children — a Father who disciplines us sometimes, to be sure, a Father who constantly has to forgive us, but a

Father too who instructs us and watches over us, and comforts and guides us, and who will never leave or forsake us. In the words of Deuteronomy, always "underneath are the everlasting arms" (Deuteronomy 33:27), or in the Psalms, our earthly father and mother may forsake us, but the Lord will take us up (Psalm 27:10). We can therefore enter into the first verse of our text and make it our own prayer, for like Israel, we too have known the abundance of the steadfast love of the Lord, his great goodness, and his mercy (v. 7).

Second, because God was Israel's loving Father, he suffered when his children suffered. Indeed, he not only saw but also experienced their affliction. "I have seen the affliction of my people who are in Egypt, and have heard their cry because of their taskmasters; I know their sufferings," the Lord told Moses (Exodus 3:7). The God of the Bible is no distant Ruler, dispassionately observing his children on earth, subjecting them to the twists and turns of an indifferent purpose. No. "I know their sufferings," God says. As in our text, the Lord is afflicted with our afflictions. He suffers our suffering. All through the Old Testament he identifies with his people. And so, his supreme identification comes in the flesh of his Son, who enters into our life, and who knows our temptations, our struggles, our pains, and finally our death. In Jesus Christ, born at Bethlehem, God becomes flesh and blood like we, and he takes all that we are upon himself, and is afflicted with our afflictions.

Third and finally, God carried Israel all the days of her life. And so too does he carry us in Jesus Christ, taking us through our struggles when we have no more strength to go on, preventing us from wandering into paths of temptation and evil, shielding us from the harm that surrounds us in the world, and yes, finally bearing us safely through the valley of the shadow of death, into the light and joy and eternal life of his good kingdom.

In response to the love of such a God who has come to us at Christmastime, let us never be like those in the verse that follows our text who rebel and grieve his Holy Spirit (v. 10). And let us join in the praise from our text for the abundance of God's steadfast covenant love, for the mercy that he has showered upon us in his Son, and for his great goodness.

37

New Year's Day

Ecclesiastes 3:1-13

I cry at weddings. I don't know if that's true of others of you in the congregation, but somehow, that is a ceremony so packed with emotion and beautiful memories that it always brings me to tears. I even cried at my own wedding, not because I was sad, but because I was filled with joy. Usually, however, weddings are not occasions for tears. They are occasions for celebration.

Similarly, we do not often think of funerals as times for laughter. Yet, I have known persons who have gotten uncontrollable giggles at a funeral service. When they should be sad, they are laughing.

There are appropriate times to do or to say things. We probably all have had the experience of speaking out, when we should have been silent, or of being silent when we should have spoken, and of "kicking ourselves" afterwards for what we have done. Everything has its appropriate time, and that is what our lesson from Ecclesiastes is saying.

The book of Ecclesiastes is part of the Wisdom literature that is found in the Bible, and it shares the common doctrine of creation that is found in Wisdom writings. That doctrine holds that God has created certain orders in the universe — customary ways in which nature and human beings behave. Those orders have been discovered by those who observe the world carefully, and if a person lives in harmony with such orders, that person is wise. But if a person will not accord with the orders God has established, that person is a fool and will not find a good life.

For example, God's order for marriage is that it be a faithful, lifelong relationship, but if one of the partners indulges in adultery, the marriage cannot be good or happy or lasting.

So God has given us the order of time, and part of wisdom is knowing when some action or word is appropriate and when it is not. There is even a time to kill, says our text — perhaps when you discover a rat in your basement. And there is a time for war — when a maniac named Adolf Hitler is killing six million Jews in gas ovens. There is a time to be born, and God has set the nine month schedule of that. But there is also a time to die, and that determination should also be left in the hands of our sovereign Creator, without interference from harried doctors or assisted suicide or extreme and futile medical measures. We are not the lords of life and death. God is. And there is indeed an appropriate time when we should give up our life to him.

But there is also a time, good Christians, when we should think about our deaths, and perhaps at the beginning of this new year, this is the time to do that. "So teach us to number our days," prays the Psalmist, "that we may get a heart of wisdom" (Psalm 90:12). As our text says, God has put eternity into our minds, although the author of Ecclesiastes thinks that we can know nothing further about that. But because of the death and resurrection of Jesus Christ, we know there is an eternal life beyond the grave. And perhaps as we examine our living at the beginning of this new year, we need to ask ourselves if what we are doing and saying will lead to that eternal life, or will it lead to the grave's extinction. We have set before us a time of decision — an appropriate time — a time to turn our lives around and to trust and obey our Lord Jesus Christ, in order that we may inherit that good and eternal life that he has won for us. "O Lord, so teach us to number our days that we may get a heart of wisdom."

Lutheran Option — Numbers 6:22-27

According to the priestly writers of the Old Testament, from whom this text comes, priests in ancient Israel had many duties. They could judge a sacrifice to be acceptable or unacceptable. They could make atonement for the sins of the people. And, as here in our text, they could lay God's blessing upon the gathered congregation of worshipers. Thus, our clergy practice of blessing a congregation at the end of a worship service comes from a tradition that dates back thousands of years, perhaps to the time of Moses and Aaron.

But we have tended to trivialize that benediction. We rarely use the form that is given us here in Numbers, sometimes introducing benedictions that have very little to do with God and that simply assure the congregation that they can be happy. "May the Lord bless you real good." "God loves you and so do I." Such are the frequent well-wishes that we hear. To be sure, many of our blessings are quoted from the Apostle Paul, and given in the name of Jesus Christ, which is quite appropriate.

We need to realize, however, what we are doing when we bless the congregation. As our text says, we are rendering to the congregation the protection ("keep you"), the gracious favor ("make his face to shine;" "lift up his countenance"), and the peace granted by God. But those are not merely wishes. When the priests blessed Israel, the priests were the channels of God's active work upon the congregation. Not mere words were being said. Rather, the very vitality and action of God was being poured out upon the people. Through the priest's human words, God's power was being communicated to the gathered folk.

As a result, the ancient priests lifted up their hands over the people, because in the Bible, hands and arms are a symbol of power (cf. the story of Moses and Aaron in Exodus 17:8-13). To celebrate a victory by God, therefore, the Psalmist sang, "His right hand and his holy arm have gotten him victory" (Psalm 98:1). Thus the arms lifted up and the hands outstretched when we say the benediction are symbols of the fact that God is pouring out his power of favor, protection, graciousness, and peace upon the people.

I have often thought, therefore, that clergy should really throw themselves into the gesture of blessing. Two or three fingers held up do not convey the proper message. The whole arms raised and the hands outstretched are much more appropriate to that which is being communicated.

We should note carefully in our text, however, that there is nothing magical about the priests' blessing. Just because a priest says the proper words and performs the proper gestures does not mean that God is bound by those. Rather, God in his freedom must

41

make the blessing effective, as we read in verse 27 of our text. And the Lord can choose to pour out his life on his people or withhold it. Nevertheless, the promise is there from God that he will indeed bless the people when the clergy pronounce God's benediction upon them, and we trust that promise. It is a holy and fearsome responsibility that we take upon ourselves when we utter God's blessing on his gathered folk.

Second Sunday after Christmas

Jeremiah 31:7-14

Jeremiah 31 is a part of what has been known as the Little Book of Comfort that is made up of chapters 30 and 31 in the Jeremiah corpus, and that announces the Lord's future salvation of the people whom he has sent into Assyrian and Babylonian exiles on account of their sin. The introduction to chapter 31, verse 1, states that the salvation is intended for both the northern and southern kingdoms of Israel, and 31:2-20 are specifically directed to the peoples of the northern kingdom. Thus, we have mention of Samaria (v. 5), Jacob (vv. 7, 11), Ephraim (vv. 6, 9, 18, 20), and Rachel (v. 15), all of the north, which fell to the Assyrians in 721 B.C. It is held by many scholars, therefore, that these are later additions to Jeremiah's ministry that covered the years from 626 to about 584 B.C. It is possible, however, that Jeremiah proclaimed salvation for the northern as well as the southern peoples of Israel.

Chapter 31:2-20 divides itself into three sections: verses 2-6, which are joined to verses 7-9 by the word "For" at the beginning of verse 7; verses 10-14; and verses 15-20. Each section envisions the future salvation of Jacob/Ephraim, their return to their land of Samaria, and then their pilgrimage to worship the Lord in Zion.

This people, states our text, is the first-born adopted son of God (v. 9). That is a familiar thought throughout the Old Testament. At the time of his deliverance of his people out of slavery in Egypt, the Lord not only freed the Israelites, but said they were his family members and adopted them as his son (cf. Hosea 11:1; Exodus 4:22-23; Jeremiah 3:19). Thus his deliverance of them from Egypt was his "redemption" of them, his "buying back" of his family member, as in Jeremiah 31:11.

The Apostle Paul draws on that terminology when he writes that we Christians have also been redeemed from our slavery, this time to sin and death, by Jesus Christ. We have been adopted as

43

God's children, he writes, so that we can call God "Abba! Father!" (Galatians 4:4-7). Our story of redemption therefore parallels Israel's, and this is our history. What, then, is the content of the salvation promised to Israel and to us? Several pictures are used in our text.

First, there is the portrayal of the salvation of those who are weak and helpless. Jeremiah states that among the remnant that will be saved are the blind and the lame, the woman with child or in travail (v. 8), and those who are captive to "hands too strong for" them (v. 11). That could be the picture of our captivity too, could it not — that we are prisoners to our sin, unable to break the bonds of the wrong that wraps itself around our lives and therefore helpless. But God promises Israel that he will free them from those who imprison them in exile, and surely God has freed us from the sin in our life that so imprisons and distorts our living by sending his Son Jesus Christ. None of us here need think our lives are hopeless. None need believe they cannot wipe out the past. God in Jesus Christ delivers us from every power that would bind and hinder our living, from every obstacle that would prevent our reunion with the Father, and we are freed to return to God's presence as his beloved children.

Second, our text portrays the gathering of the redeemed to Zion to praise and to worship God (vv. 6, 8, 12), and that of course is what we do every Sunday, isn't it? We, the redeemed children of the Lord, gather in this place where God is present to "sing aloud with gladness" and to "give praise and say, 'The Lord has saved (us) his people' " (v. 7). Now we have entrance to the presence of the living God. Now we can approach his throne with confidence, because Jesus Christ has died for our sin and opened the way to the Father.

Third, as we gather for worship and then go out from this "Zion" of ours, we can be "radiant over the goodness of the Lord," as redeemed Israel would be radiant (v. 12). For what does the Lord furnish us here in our worship and in our daily activities? Surely here in his presence, we are given not only God's forgiveness, but also his comfort for our distress and tribulations, his guidance for our decisions, his correction of our wayward ways, his directions through his Word about how to have his life and have it abundantly. Then as we go out, he accompanies us in our daily round, keeping us "as a shepherd keeps his flock," (v. 10), furnishing us with the necessities of our lives (v. 12), so that we are "like a watered garden," says our text (v. 12), tended, cared for, nourished. By the vitality of the Spirit in which God goes with us, we can blossom and bring forth fruit for his purposes. As the Psalmist sings, those who trust in the Lord and follow his ways are "... like a tree planted by streams of water, that yields its fruit in its season, and its leaf does not wither" (Psalm 1:3). For those who worship and live in the Spirit of Jesus Christ and serve him, their lives can be productive and have meaning, because they serve the purposes of God.

Fourth, we should note the characteristics of the picture of salvation given us in our text. What does it entail? Planting crops, enjoying the harvest (v. 5), dancing, having fun at a party (v. 13), basking in the satisfaction given by the goodness of the Lord (v. 14) — in short, normal, decent, enjoyable everyday life. We often think of salvation as a state of perfection in the future, and so it is in parts of the Bible (cf. 1 Corinthians 13:12). But there is also a foretaste of God's salvation in Jesus Christ given to us now — the joy and gladness of which our text speaks (v. 13), the comfort, the satisfaction of human life returned to the way God meant it to be in the beginning. A good life, a decent life, a meaningful and productive life — these are offered to us now by the work of God in his Son our Lord.

God did not give up on the Israelites whom he sent into exile because of their sin against him. And God does not give up on us either. Rather, he sent us his Son, born at Bethlehem, to redeem us and to reclaim us as his beloved children. And through that Son he offers us not only salvation in the future in his eternal kingdom. But he also offers us his goodness now, in days full of satisfaction and of joy. We have only to open our hearts and lives, in trust, to receive his amazing gifts.

Epiphany of Our Lord

Isaiah 60:1-6

Isaiah 60-62 represents a sharp contrast with what has gone before in the preceding chapters of Third Isaiah (chs. 56-66). Up to this point in Isaiah's collection are found a mixture of conditional promises, scathing judgments, warnings, and calls to repentance. But beginning in chapter 60, the tone changes and we find nothing but unconditional, soaring, lyrical proclamations of salvation. Our text forms the first six verses of that glad announcement, and is a portion of the whole poem of 60:1-22.

Here God offers his open-hearted mercy to all the inhabitants of Jerusalem, even though they have done nothing to deserve it. As is true throughout the scriptures, God's action of mercy precedes any repentance and turning on his people's part. And it is that un-merited love of God to which the remnant of Judah is asked to respond in answering love. We turn to God in love and obedience when we see with what love he has loved us in Jesus Christ. "We love because he first loved us."

Those things that are offered to the remnant of Judah in this message are no less than the gifts of the kingdom of God. In chapters 60-62, Third Isaiah pictures the coming of that kingdom, and it is in the light of that coming that Judah is asked to be faithful and obedient — not *in order that* the kingdom will come, but because it is in fact coming.

Jerusalem is addressed in verse 1 as a woman, mourning in the dust. But she is bidden to arise, because God is going to be present with her in his glory (vv. 1-2). Here, God's glory is portrayed as his shining effulgence, as his material manifestation of his Being on earth (cf. 35:2; 40:5; 58:8; 59:19; Ezekiel 1:26-28). God, whose presence is often described in terms of light, is coming to his people!

As a result, Jerusalem will shine with the reflected light of God's glory (vv. 2-3), just as Moses' face shone when he descended from talking to God on Mount Sinai (Exodus 34:29; 2 Corinthians 3:12-18). To this reflected light, all the nations, who now dwell in darkness, will be drawn (vv. 2-3), because they will realize that God is to be found with Jerusalem (cf. Zechariah 8:23; Isaiah 2:3). It is a cosmic and universal picture.

When the nations are drawn to Jerusalem, they will also bring back with them all of Israel's exiled children who have been scattered throughout the world (v. 4; cf. v. 9), and so Judah's heart will swell with joy (v. 5), like that of a mother's exulting over the return of her lost children.

The nations will not only come to Jerusalem to return Israel's lost children, however. They will also come up to Jerusalem to worship the Lord. They will bring their treasures to be used in rebuilding the ruined temple (vv. 5-7), and they will bring their animals to be offered as sacrifices upon the altar (vv. 6-7). There will be caravans of camels bringing gifts from the southwest desert tribes of Midian and Ephah; gold and frankincense from the Arabian trading center of Seba; herds from Kedar and Nabaioth, famous for their sheep and rams; silver and gold from the sea peoples; fine timber from the North (vv. 6, 9, 13). All will be used to pay homage to the one Lord of all.

In short, what we find in these six introductory sentences to this poem is a picture of the reversal of the fortunes of Judah, which is, in Third Isaiah's time, a struggling little subprovince of the Persian Empire, scratching out an existence among the ruins of Jerusalem. The prophet proclaims that there will be the return of her God to her in forgiveness and mercy, the light of God's salvation shone upon her, the pilgrimage of all nations to Jerusalem, with their treasures, to worship the one God who is seen as Lord of them all. Such is the promise for the future coming of his universal kingdom that the Lord holds out to his struggling and suffering people.

Obviously, this text from Third Isaiah has been designated for the celebration of Epiphany, because it mentions that gold and frankincense will be brought by the foreign nations to honor God (v. 6). According to Matthew 2:11, those are two of the gifts that the astrologers from the East brought to the infant Jesus, and perhaps

Matthew understands those gifts as a fulfillment of this Isaiah prophecy. But that connection between our text and Matthew has many implications.

First, the presence of God with his covenant people, of which the church is now a part, is understood to be found in the birth of Jesus. God has indeed come to us in his Son. This Word of Third Isaiah has become flesh in Jesus Christ, who dwells among us by his Spirit. And we, like Judah in our text, are totally undeserving of that favor. We, too, have been disobedient and unrepentant, but God in his overwhelming mercy has nevertheless come to us in his incarnation, offering his abundant love to which we are called to respond in answering love.

Second, in Jesus Christ, the glory of the Lord has shone upon us, as Jerusalem was promised. "For it is the God who said, 'Let light shine out of darkness,' " writes Paul, "who has shone in our hearts to give the light of the knowledge of the glory of God in the face of Christ" (2 Corinthians 4:6). The full effulgence of our glorious God is veiled in the flesh of our Lord.

Third, as followers of our Lord, we are to reflect that glorious presence, as Jerusalem in our text would reflect it. "You are the light of the world," Jesus taught us (Matthew 5:14). But our light is not our own. It is the reflection of the light of Jesus Christ, who by his Spirit lives and works within and through us (cf. Galatians 2:20). And we are to reflect Christ's life, Christ's glory, in everything we do and say.

Fourth, if we truly reflect the love and life of Christ in our lives, then indeed, the nations of the world will be drawn to that light. For "I, when I am lifted up from the earth, will draw all people to myself," Jesus promised (John 12:32). If we lift up the death of Jesus on the cross, and his resurrection, if we shine forth with his glorious love for all, all nations everywhere will be drawn to come to him and to worship him as the one Lord of their lives.

Fifth and finally, all of these things, Third Isaiah promised, would come to pass in the Kingdom of God. And with the birth of our Lord, that kingdom has in fact begun to break into our world. God's abundant and eternal life, promised to his people, has now intervened in our history. And while its fullness is not yet realized, it has begun and will come to be. So we can join in the announcement of the prophet on this day of Epiphany. "Arise, shine!" all you Christian people, "for your light has come, and the glory of the Lord has risen upon you!"

Baptism of Our Lord

Isaiah 42:1-9

The lectionary often begins a reading at the end of one poem and includes the beginning of another. Such is the case here. Isaiah 42:1-4 forms the climactic last stanza of the long poem concerning the trial with the nations that begins in 41:1. Isaiah 42:5-9 is the opening stanza of the poem that encompasses 42:5-17. Thus, we will initially deal with 42:1-4 and then 42:5-9.

Isaiah 42:1-4 is the first of the well-known Servant Songs in Second Isaiah. It immediately raises the question: "Who is the Servant?" There have been years of scholarly discussion about the question, but in my view and that of many others, the Servant represents corporate Israel, as in 41:9 and 44:1-2. However, the Servant is not Israel in Babylonian exile, as she actually is. Rather, the Servant is Israel as she is meant to be, Israel as the Lord will transform her to be, Israel as God will use her in his future salvation of the nations.

It is exceedingly important to realize therefore that Jesus Christ in the New Testament becomes the embodiment of the Servant, summing up in his incarnate person all that Israel was meant by God to be. For example, Christ becomes the Son of God, called out of Egypt (Matthew 2:15), as Israel was the called adopted son (cf. Hosea 11:1), and Christ is the true vine (John 15:1), as Israel was the vine (Psalm 80:7). Christ is not a replacement for Israel, but rather is the corporate personality, the fulfillment and summing up, of the intended Israel of the Old Testament, continuing God's work of salvation across the centuries. His connection with Israel is not to be overlooked by the preacher. In the Old Testament, God chooses Israel as his Servant to carry out his purpose, and Jesus of Nazareth becomes, in the New Testament, that Servant. The witness to God's work is continuous across the two testaments, and God's one purpose of salvation runs through the whole biblical story.

Because our Lord Christ became the Servant, the description of him, given in Isaiah 42:1-4, is exceedingly important for us. Obviously this Isaiah text has been chosen as the stated lesson for this Sunday when we celebrate the baptism of our Lord, because it says that God has put his Spirit upon his Servant, and it is at his baptism that the Spirit descends from heaven upon Jesus (cf. the gospel lesson). Thus, Jesus the Servant is "chosen" by God, is upheld by God, and is a delight to God — all stated in 42:1, that parallels 41:9.

According to 42:1-4, then, the primary work of the Servant is to establish God's "justice," God's *mispat*, in all the world. Three times the word appears in these four verses. And here it could properly be read as God's "rule," God's sovereignty over all the earth. The nations are called to trial in Isaiah 41:1-29, and the final verdict of the court in 42:1-4 is that God's rule, God's order for life, will be the governance that the Servant will establish throughout the earth, enabled by the Spirit of God given to him (cf. Isaiah 11:2-4). It is no accident, therefore, that Jesus comes preaching the Kingdom or the Kingship of God. God's way will become the rule of life for all nations.

The Servant will not establish God's rule by force of arms, however, nor will persuasive public preaching be his main role (v. 2). Rather, his mercy toward the "bruised reeds" — the hurting of this world — and his tenderness for those whose lives are almost extinguished like a sputtering wick will be his modes of expression (v. 3) — surely motifs that found their fulfillment in Jesus' forgiveness and healing and sacrifice for us all upon the cross.

Verse 4 of our poem then picks up the words "bruised" and "burn dimly" from verse 3, and uses them in the Hebrew to say that the Servant will neither fail ("be bruised") nor be discouraged ("burn dimly"). The time of his work may be long and the obstacles to his ministry be great, with only a slim chance of success, but nevertheless, the Servant will prevail and finally establish God's rule over all. In New Testament terms, the kingdom will in fact come and God's order for human life will indeed be established. Such is the promise to us of both Old and New Testaments.

Verse 5 of 42:5-9 begins a new poem and opens with the hymnic praise of the Creator of the world. This God, who sends his Servant to us, is able to establish his rule because he is the powerful Maker who spread out (literally, "beat out to a thin surface") the vastness of the heavens, who laid out the earth upon the waters, and who gave his animating breath to all humans and creatures (cf. Psalm 104:29-30; Genesis 2:7). The God of history is also the Almighty Creator of all — a frequent note in Second Isaiah.

But that Almighty Lord is also the King who, in his Son, has "emptied himself, taking the form of a servant" (Philippians 2:7), and that Servant is called "in righteousness," that is, in God's will to save. ("Righteousness," throughout the Bible, is the fulfillment of the demands of a relationship.) God guides the Servant by the hand and keeps him. And then God gives the Servant as a "covenant to the people" (v. 6). In short, Jesus Christ is God's pledge to us of his presence with us and of his salvation of us. He is "the light" for us and for all peoples, shining in our present darkness (cf. Isaiah 9:2; John 1:4-9; 8:12, et al.). He is the one who can liberate humanity from its bondage to the world's forces and to sin and death (v. 7).

There is no doubt about it. The God who has sent the Servant, Jesus Christ, is the one and only Lord (v. 8). There is no other god besides him, no other deity who is glorious in might and love, no other god who is to be praised and worshiped. And as in the New Testament, the Servant of the one true God, Jesus Christ, is the one way to God and the incarnation of God's truth and of God's very Person (John 14:6).

As evidence of the sole lordship of God, Second Isaiah frequently points to God's rule over the span of history. In the court case with the nations (41:22), the Lord challenges the nations' gods to tell what is going to take place in history. But of course they cannot do so, because only the Holy One of Israel rules over all the events of time. So, too, here in verse 9, God points to the fact that he has foretold what has happened in the past. He has promised, and it has come true. He has decreed, and it has taken place.

Now, in Second Isaiah's present, God promises a new act of salvation to come. As in Isaiah 43:19, exiled Israel is to look not to

53

the saving acts of the Lord in the past, but to another new act of salvation that will deliver her from Babylonian exile, while that deed will at the same time gather up all of God's past promises and bring them to completion (cf. Isaiah 40:8; 55:10-11). It is for that new saving act that Israel is to wait (Isaiah 40:31).

Certainly Israel of the sixth century B.C. was released from Babylonian exile by Cyrus of Persia, as promised by Second Isaiah (45:1, 13). But the new age of God's order did not find its complete fulfillment in Second Isaiah's time through the instrument of the Servant Israel. Instead, we have to look to the final Servant, to Jesus Christ, whose forgiveness, mercy, and liberation are indeed being proclaimed to all nations. Through Christ's continuing work in our world, he is bringing in God's promised kingdom. Through him, God is establishing his world-wide rule that will finally cover the earth as the waters cover the sea.

Second Sunday after Epiphany

Isaiah 49:1-7

This is the second of the Servant Songs found in the prophecies of Second Isaiah, from the sixth century B.C. (See the discussion for last Sunday.) As such, it represents Israel's reflection on her call to be the Lord's Servant. The Servant speaks in verses 1-5, the Lord's words are given in verses 6 and 7.

This text can be read in several ways. First, it can be taken as a description solely of a new, transformed Israel's role in the service of God. Second, it can mirror the prophet's own ministry, with its call, its failures and discouragements, its source of strength and encouragement in God, and its mission to the nations. From that point of view, probably every clergy person can identify with its words. But third, the text can be applied to every Christian. Every member of the church is called to be a servant and evangel or missionary for the Lord, spreading the gospel both near and far. And it is this latter interpretation that I shall use in this discussion.

"The Lord called me from the womb" (v. 1). The scriptures have the profound understanding that God creates each child in the mother's womb for a purpose. Certainly that was Jeremiah's understanding (Jeremiah 1:5) and the Apostle Paul's (Galatians 1:15). But that is true not only of such special prophets and apostles, but also of each one of us. God makes us for a purpose, for a place in his plan, carefully knitting us together with bones and sinews (Job 10:11), shaping each of our individual body forms and DNA and physical and mental capabilities, in order that he may use us to work out his will in the world. We are "called" individuals, intended for a role in God's work.

Then, says our text, God names us (v. 1). And of course that is what happens in our baptisms. We are given our Christian names and declared to be God's children, belonging to him and to no other. He gives us his family name, Christian, and makes us a part of his household, as his beloved son or daughter. From that time on, we belong to God's covenant people, and we live and move and have our being always in relationship with our Lord.

Like Israel and Jesus' disciples and all of the Christians who have gone before us, as we grow in the faith, we are given God's Word. Spoken to us by our parents, our church teachers, in sermon and scripture, in anthem and in hymn, the Word of God is entrusted to us to make our own and to tell to all near and far. And that word is by no means a mean and insignificant gift. No, it is a powerful word. As Hebrews says, "The Word of God is living and active, sharper than any two-edged sword, piercing to the division of soul and spirit ... and discerning the thoughts and intentions of the heart" (Hebrews 4:12). The Word of God is so powerful, says the prophet Jeremiah, that it is like a burning fire (Jeremiah 20:9) or like a hammer that breaks rock in pieces (Jerermiah 23:29). In short, this Word of God given to us has a power within it to change the lives of those to whom we speak it, and to make of them new persons in Jesus Christ. Thus, we can have great expectations as we spread the Word of the gospel in our homes or occupations or social circles or through our missions. We can expect the Word of God to have an effect on human lives. And indeed, it often has. We could give many illustrations of that working of God's Word.

We could also give illustrations of many times when the Word of God has seemed to have no effect, however, and when all of our efforts to spread the gospel and to enlarge the church have come to nought. Certainly, most preachers could tell you of those times, and we have only to read the morning headlines to feel a sense of failure and discouragement. As our text says, we could mourn that "I have labored in vain, I have spent my strength for nothing and vanity" (v. 4). After all, our society is full of violence and greed, evil deeds and wrong unchecked, and the Word of God that the church has been speaking for years has not seemed to make a dent in society's ways.

Yet, our text for the morning tells us three things in the midst of our discouragement. First, God has us "hid" (vv. 2 and 3). As Colossians says, our lives are hid in Christ with God (Colossians 3:3). That is, we are protected by our Lord from the forces of evil that would battle against our mission as God's servants. Second, our "right is with the Lord, and (our) recompense is with God" (v. 4). That means that our judgment and the judgment of anyone else concerning our success or failure as servants and disciples of the Lord are meaningless (cf. 1 Corinthians 4:1-4). Society may laugh at our efforts to be the Lord's servants as it laughed at Jesus dying on the cross. But God knew what he was working out by that death on Golgotha, and he knows what he is accomplishing through our work. It may seem futile and without effect to us. But God alone judges its effectiveness, and he brings forth from our labors the fruit that he desires. And so, third, we can say with our text, "My God has become my strength" (v. 5). In him, our work for the gospel is not in vain (cf. 1 Corinthians 15:58).

Indeed, the surprising note in answer to the discouragement that is voiced in our text is that God gives his servant an even greater mission and harder work to do (cf. Jeremiah 12:5, 6). The faithful in Israel are called not only to bring their own society back to God, but they are also commanded to go into all the world and to make disciples of all nations. It is as if God is saying to us in so many words, "You think your attempts to live and spread the gospel are in vain where you are. All right. I'll give you an even bigger job. Spread the gospel throughout the world so that all peoples everywhere may be saved." And you see, that can be said because the work of the Lord and our mission in it depend not on our strength, not on our resources, not on our abilities, but on the strength and unlimited vitality and unconquerable love found in God. God is Lord of this world and all beyond it. He is the Holy One (v. 7), unlike any other. And his might and his life and his love cannot be defeated by any of the ways of this wayward world. So our text says to us, in that light, "Get to work. Trust God. Spread his Word. It will bear fruit in God's good time."

The final stanza of our text, verse 7, gives its affirmation of that final triumph of the Lord. For it pictures all kings and princes, all nations of the earth, bringing their worship and paying their homage to the one Lord of all. And of course, that is the reassurance given to all of us servants too, isn't it? There will come a day when every knee bows and every tongue confesses that Jesus Christ is Lord, to the glory of God the Father (Philippians 2:10-11). And to those of us who are faithful servants, our Lord himself will say, "Well done, good and faithful servant ... Enter into the joy of your master" (Matthew 25:21).

Third Sunday after Epiphany

Isaiah 9:1-4

Isaiah 9:1-4 is the first part of the lesson that is the stated Old Testament text for a Sunday on Christmas Eve. But on that Sunday, all of 9:2-7 is sometimes read. This time only the first stanza of the oracle is prescribed.

Obviously, 9:1-4 has been specified because it is paired with the Gospel reading in Matthew 4:12-23, and because portions of verses 1 and 2 are quoted from the Septuagint version in that Matthew passage. After the death of John the Baptist, when Jesus leaves Nazareth and goes to Capernaum to "dwell," Matthew understands that as a fulfillment of Isaiah 9:1-2. Jesus is the Savior who brings "great light" into the lives of those in Gentile Galilee, just as he is the Savior who brings light and release for us Gentiles who sit in the shadow of darkness and of death.

The result of Jesus' coming into our lives is to give us great rejoicing, joy equal to that of those who celebrate an abundant harvest or to that of those who exult over a great victory over an enemy (Isaiah 9:3). And that joy comes from the fact that our Lord has, indeed, lifted the "yoke" from our shoulders, and broken the "rod" of that which oppresses us.

In the Old Testament, there are many references to a "yoke." Any forms of captivity or subjection to another are frequently described as "yokes." Thus, Israel's slavery in Egypt was a "yoke" (Leviticus 26:13), as is Judah's defeat and subjugation to Babylonia (Jeremiah 27:8, 11, etc.). And when the Lord delivers Israel from bondage by the exodus from Egypt, Leviticus says that the Lord has broken the bars of Israel's yoke and made her walk erect (Leviticus 26:13).

"Yoke," however, can also signify God's guidance of his people. The indictment that God looses against Judah in Jeremiah declares, "Long ago you broke your yoke and burst your bonds; and you said, 'I will not serve' " (Jeremiah 2:20). That means that a life faithful to God is guided by a Master, who holds its reins and directs it in the right way. The biblical life of faith is not unbridled freedom, but obedience to a guiding Lord. Jesus therefore bids us to "take my yoke upon you and learn from me; for I am gentle and lowly in heart, and you will find rest for your souls. For my yoke is easy and my burden is light" (Matthew 11:29-30).

In order to lead us in the right paths, God first, however, must free us from our captivity to other powers of this world. That is the liberation celebrated in our text for the morning; Zebulon and Naphtali will be delivered from their captivity to Assyria by a messianic, davidic king (vv. 6-7). But the Gospel reading in Matthew spiritualizes that to a certain extent and declares that Jesus is that Messiah who delivers not only Zebulon and Naphtali, but also us from our captivity, from the "yokes" that burden us.

What are our burdening "yokes"? Third Isaiah says that they are yokes of wickedness (Isaiah 58:6), burdens that oppress us, and indeed they are, are they not? — the sins that bend our lives out of shape daily; the burdens of guilt that weigh us down from the past; foolish prides and uncaring self-interest; indifference toward the plight of our neighbors and greedy grasping after our own well-being; repeated forgetfulness of our God and failure to practice his love and forgiveness; and yes, finally, our fear of the loneliness and pain of death and the meaninglessness that the grave can give to every human life. Sin and death hold us captive and subject us to their "yoke."

But the announcement of our Isaiah text is that our Messiah has broken the yokes that burden us, snapping in two the bonds of sin and freeing us for new and good lives, defeating the bars of death that would keep us forever locked in its shadowy and decaying depths. And so we, like those Galileans of our text can rejoice with exceeding great joy, because we have been freed for a new life in Jesus Christ our Lord.

That the Gospel according to Matthew understands our Lord Jesus as the fulfillment of this Old Testament text points to the ongoing work of God that binds the two testaments together. Throughout Matthew, we find the phrase, "This was to fulfill...."

This was to fulfill what was spoken by the prophet. This was to fulfill what God declared to Israel in the days of the Israel of the Old Testament. In other words, God began a history of salvation in the time of Old Testament Israel, and that history continues into the New Testament and finds its fulfillment in Jesus Christ.

God made lots of promises to Israel, and one of them is found here in Isaiah 9. God promises light in our darkness, freedom from our bondage, joy instead of our sorrow. And the God of the biblical history is the God who always keeps his word. As Second Isaiah proclaimed, God's Word stands forever (Isaiah 40:8). When he speaks his Word, it does not come to nothing, it does not fall by the wayside, it does not return to God void. Rather, God's Word, says Second Isaiah, is like the rain and the snow that come down from heaven "and return not thither but water the earth, making it bring forth and sprout, giving seed to the sower and bread to the eater" (Isaiah 55:10). God's Word brings results. It works in human lives until it is fulfilled. And so when God promised, according to our text, that the people who walked in darkness would see a great light and have the yoke of oppression and captivity removed from them, the Lord God worked through all the centuries until he sent his Son, our Messiah, to fulfill the ancient words that God through Isaiah had promised. And now you and I, we Gentiles, can find ourselves released from the yokes that oppress us — from our sin and from the finality of death — if we trust God's fulfillment of Isaiah's promise in Jesus Christ our Lord. More than that, God's saving work in our lives continues, stretching out toward the future, bringing to pass God's further promises given us by our Lord Jesus.

So let us rejoice, good Christians, like those who rejoice at an abundant harvest, like those who celebrate a glorious victory. For our God in Jesus Christ has indeed won the victory, and we, like Israel, are his people.

Fourth Sunday after Epiphany

Micah 6:1-8

The important thing to remember about this text from Micah is that it represents a court case between Israel and the Lord. God is the plaintive in the judicial procedure, Israel is the defendant, and the hills, mountains, and foundations of the earth are the jury. God, the plaintive, presents his case in verses 3-5, Israel, the defendant, replies in verses 6-7, and verse 8 is the verdict that confirms God's position and judges Israel for what she should have done but has not done.

The Lord's most telling accusation against his people is that they have been weary with him (v. 3). God recounts, in verses 4-5, all of his saving acts on behalf of his covenant people in the past. He has delivered them out of slavery in Egypt, given them his guidance in the law and led them safely through the terrors of the wilderness, prevented Balaam from bringing a deadly curse upon them, and brought them through the Jordan from Shittim to their first encampment in the promised land at Gilgal.

Yet despite all of God's loving deeds toward his people in their past history, they have forgotten what God has done. They have not kept that memory of the sacred history that gives a people gratitude and hope for the future and patience in the midst of tribulation (surely a three-point sermon). Instead, Israel, like so many in our time, is just weary with God — weary of her constant pleading with him and inability to find him. She is in some kind of trouble, and she wants God to bail her out, but God has not answered or helped, and Israel is disgusted with him.

What does it take to call this unresponsive deity to her aid? Israel asks (vv. 6-7). Should she sacrifice burnt offerings to him of calves a year old that are so much more valuable than newborns? Would God be satisfied with thousands of rams, as Solomon offered him (1 Kings 8:63), or with literal rivers of precious olive oil used for food and healing? Or maybe, the disgusted speaker says sarcastically, God would like Israel to offer those child sacrifices forbidden in the law (Leviticus 18:21; 20:2-5; Deuteronomy 18:10) and condemned by the prophets as pagan practices (Jeremiah 7:31, et al.). What does it take to appease an implacable deity? That is Israel's exasperated question.

The answer is given in the words of God's prophetic spokesman in verse 8 — an answer that condemns Israel. God has shown his covenant people what is good, and he has shown all of us what is good and what we are to do, for his reply is addressed to "O man," "O *'adam*" in the Hebrew, meaning "humankind." The Lord has shown all of us what he requires of us. He has not left us to stumble around in the dark, making up the rules as we go along, and searching vainly to find the proper paths for our lives. No. God has guided us, and he says very plainly how he expects us to act.

First of all, reads our text, God wants us to do "justice," *mispat*. That can refer to legal justice, and certainly our society is often lacking in just courts of law. But while the meaning of "justice" in this passage includes judicial equity, it is also much broader than that. *Mispat* means to establish God's order in every area of life — in our nation and society, our towns and homes. God wants every relationship of life structured and conducted according to his will, given us through the scriptures — permeated with his love, his fairness, his forgiveness, his mercy, his straight and upright truth.

Second, our text says that what God requires of us is "to love kindness," but once again, the meaning goes beyond our understanding of those words. The term for "kindness" in the Hebrew is *hesed*, which is a covenant term. It means to be faithful to our covenant with God and with one another, to be bound together in solidarity with them, to be a community that lives in steadfast loyalty to God and to other human beings. And we are to love those ties — love our relation with our Lord who has made us in his image, love our relation with our neighbors for whom we are always responsible. Thus, faithful covenant solidarity with God and all those around us is not understood as a duty here in our text, but as a pleasure, rendered in lovingkindness, because God has first loved us.

Finally, Israel is told in our text that she is expected to walk "humbly" with her God. While that meaning eschews all proud self-righteousness and self-will, the word for "humbly" is *hasene'a* in the Hebrew, that has the meaning of "attentively," "paying attention to," "watching." We are to walk "attentively" with our God, not in proud self-independence as so many of us desire, but paying attention always to what God wants. We are to watch him for what is good, seeking after his will and not our own, being alert to his guidance and commands for the way we conduct our lives. Through sermon and scripture, prayer and meditation, we are to be intent on God's guidance of our steps and future. And if we do that, then it will become possible also to "do justice" and "love *hesed.*" The first two requirements rest on the third — to seek always after our God, in every relationship of our daily round.

The prophet Micah, throughout his book, is sure that Israel never lives up to these requirements laid upon her by her Lord. And of course we never live up to them either, do we? All by ourselves, with our own strength and will, we repeatedly do not rely in all things upon our Lord.

But within the book of Micah, there is also the promise of a Messiah, come from Bethlehem Ephrathah (5:2-4) — a Messiah whose birth we celebrated a few short weeks ago at Christmas. According to our gospel lesson from Matthew 5, that Messiah once again laid these requirements of God upon us, when he gave his Sermon on the Mount. And his requirements and these of Micah seem impossible for us to meet — as they are, indeed, if the Messiah has left us on our own.

But the gospel, the good news, of course, is that he has not left us to depend upon our own devices and wills to satisfy the requirements of our God. Instead, Jesus Christ has forgiven us all our sins and shortcomings by his death and resurrection. And then, he has sent his Spirit into our hearts, transforming our lives and giving us the willpower and ability to do the good that we are required by God to do. We do not earn our way into the favor of the Lord, good Christians — not by multitudes of sacrifices, as Micah says. Rather, God accepts us as "good" because of the sacrifice of Jesus Christ. And then he enables us to do the "good" by the power of his Holy

65

Spirit. Our responsibility is to trust that God in Jesus Christ can, in fact, work that transformation in our lives. For as Christ works in us, we will, indeed, find that we do justice, and love kindness, and walk humbly with our God.

Fifth Sunday after Epiphany

Isaiah 58:1-9a (9b-12)

In the church, we speak often of "salvation." But what do we mean by that term? Certainly several different meanings are given us in the scriptures. The Apostle Paul understood "salvation" to include our resurrection from the dead, our vindication in Christ at the last judgment, and our entrance into the eternal Kingdom of God. And certainly Third Isaiah's understanding is preparatory for that, for in this sixth century B.C. prophetic text, "salvation" means to live abundantly in God's presence.

In verses 8-12 of our text, that meaning is spelled out. God's presence with the faithful will mean light that dispenses every shadow (vv. 8a, 10cd) — light that will "break forth," like flood water bursting out to cover the earth (v. 8a). God's presence will give "healing" to every hurt (v. 8b) and protection and guidance in every circumstance (vv. 8cd; 11a). Fellowship with him will mean renewed vitality and productivity, like that given to a watered garden (v. 11c). It will enable persons to rebuild the ruins of their lives (v. 12), and to know God's immediate fellowship with them (v. 9). When the faithful call to God, he will answer them; they will cry to him, and he will reply, "Here I am!" like a father responding to the call of a searching child (v. 9). Yes, that is a central meaning of the word "salvation" — to be with God and to enjoy life abundant in his presence — and I suppose every one of us would like thus to be saved.

Certainly the Judeans to whom our prophetic passage is spoken would like to have such a life. They are returnees with their families from Babylonian exile, and their plight is rather desperate. Their city of Jerusalem lies still in ruins; they are plagued with crop shortages and inflation and lack of housing; and there is dissension between their priestly Zadokite leaders and the Levitical priests who remained in Palestine during the exile. In fact, most of

Third Isaiah comes from the Levites and their followers who were persecuted and deprived of priestly duties by the Zadokite priests when the latter returned from Babylonia after 538 B.C.

The Judean populace and their Zadokite priests therefore are pictured in our text as seeking the salvation of God by undergoing a day of fast and penitence. They go through all the rituals of such a day, crying out in prayer to God, falling prostrate on the ground, rending their garments, sprinkling ashes on their heads, donning sackcloth, and foregoing normal activities (cf. Joshua 7:6; 1 Kings 21:27; Psalm 35:13-14, etc.). They are a very religious people, who "seek" God daily, that is, they ask the prophets for oracles from God in order to know how to walk according to his will (v. 2a). And they imagine that if they go through the proper rituals of penance, God will take notice of them and come to be with them in his saving presence. They cannot understand why that has not been so. They are very much like us modern churchgoers who believe that our attendance in worship will guarantee God's salvation of us.

As a result, the prophet adopts the role of a prophetic "watchman" for the people to warn them that their life is in danger from God (v. 1; cf. Ezekiel 33:1-9). And he announces that God has not listened to their prayers and taken heed of their plight and come to dwell with them, because they really have not been praying to God and offering true repentance and seeking to walk in his commandments (vv. 3c-5). In reality, they have forsaken God (v. 2d).

Instead, the Judeans have been using fast days to pursue business as usual (= the meaning of "seek your own pleasure," v. 3c), when fast days were supposed to be times of rest from labor (Leviticus 16:29, 31). And far from repenting of sin, the people quarrel and fight and oppress one another (v. 4). So God does not listen to them. We have the old stereotypical saying that "God hears every prayer," but not according to the prophets (cf. also Isaiah 1:15). Persons who pray must be "acceptable to the Lord" (v. 5c).

What pleases God? Surely not phony religiosity and prayer that is contradicted by our actions. No. Third Isaiah spells out part of the answer in 6-9b, 9c-12. The repentance that God chooses and the worship that is pleasing to him is the worship or "work" (for the word for "worship" in both Old and New Testament means

68

"work") — the work of liberation, the removal of every yoke that binds human beings to any sort of servitude (vv. 6, 9c). And within his definition of servitude, Third Isaiah includes the bondage or oppression of the poor that is incurred by debt and that is mentioned so often by the prophets (v. 6b; cf. Amos 2:6-8; Jeremiah 34:8-9). But in our text, Third Isaiah also speaks of slavery to the gnawing pain of an empty stomach (vv. 7a, 10a), and to the misery of homelessness and exclusion from the community (v. 7b). He talks of the shivering shame of being dressed in rags (v. 7cd) and of the sin of withholding help from our "own flesh," that is, from those with whom we share a common humanity as brothers and sisters under God (v. 7d). And in verse 9cd, the prophet also mentions the wickedness spoken by the Zadokite party against the Levites, but of course, "speaking wickedness" could refer to all our gossip and evil talk and lies about our neighbors. Such sins prevent our true service of God and mark our worship and repentance as phony before him, and so they cut us off from that salvation, that presence of God with us, that we would so much like to have.

Before we label all of that as "works-righteousness," let us remember that our Lord Jesus announces to us the same message — that mercy toward others is good in God's sight, because it is finally mercy toward him. "Truly, I say to you, as you did it to one of the least of these my brethren, you did it to me" (Matthew 25:40). Love toward our fellow human beings is finally love toward God in Jesus Christ, and true love of God always issues in love toward our neighbors. Apart from that, the repentance we mouth and the worship we carry out is rather futile, as our text says.

To be sure, all of us sin and fall sort of the glory of God. All of us fail in our love for our neighbors and therefore in our love for God. And that is why we come into this church and offer our confessions of sin. We all ultimately have only the one prayer, "God, be merciful to me, a sinner" (Luke 18:13). And our Lord tells us that the God of mercy hears that prayer and justifies us in his sight by the cross and resurrection of Jesus Christ.

But what our text further reminds us this morning is that even that prayer must be followed by merciful action in our everyday lives. We cannot just confess our sin and then do nothing to aid others. No. Confession — true confession — leads to deeds of mercy in our society, and kindness toward our associates, and acts of forgiveness and self-sacrifice in our homes, and efforts every morning to do those things that are pleasing to our God. The work of worship and the work of daily life must coincide. And from that work, we will be able sincerely to call, and God will answer us, "Here I am!"

Transfiguration Sunday

Exodus 24:12-18

It seems clear that we have a different source beginning in verse 12 than that found in 24:1-11, because while Moses and the elders are already on Mount Sinai in verse 11, Moses is bidden to ascend the mountain in verse 12. Nevertheless, the context forms a continuous story. The covenant of God with Israel is "cut" in 24:3-8, followed by the account of what could be called the first Lord's Supper in 24:9-11. Moses and the priests and the elders eat and drink the covenant meal with God himself. Then, following our text, God gives instructions to Moses and Israel about how to build the tabernacle with its ark of the covenant and all of its accoutrements (Exodus 25-31). Yet, it is also implied by 24:12 and by 32:18; 33:19; and chapter 34, that the instructions that God writes on the tables of the law given to Moses include the commandments now found in the Decalogue and the Ritual Decalogue of 34:12-28.

Obviously this text in Exodus 24 has been chosen for this Sunday of the Transfiguration because it speaks of the glory of the Lord descending on Mount Sinai "like a devouring fire" (v. 17). "The glory of the Lord" refers here, in verse 16, to that shining light effulgence by which God manifests himself on earth, and it reminds the reader of the Transfiguration in which Jesus' face shines like the sun and his garments become white as light. The glory of the Lord, who made the light and the sun, can manifest their brilliance, and so human beings must be protected from that dazzling light by a cloud (vv. 15-16). Indeed, in the New Testament, even the reflection of such light must be veiled from the sight of those who view it (cf. 2 Corinthians 3:7, 13). As 1 Timothy 6:16 says, God dwells in "unapproachable light," and in John, Jesus Christ is "the light and the life of" all (John 1:4). The incredible gift, therefore, is that humankind has been allowed to approach the very light of God in the incarnation of our Lord.

71

There is a further emphasis to be noted in our text for the morning, however, and that is contained in 24:12. God specifically tells Moses that the covenant people must receive their instructions for their living from the Lord and not from human beings, not even Moses. In other words, the people of God are to live by the Lord's law and commandments and not by the ways and ordinances of the world and the society around them (cf. Leviticus 18:1-4).

Now we know that there can be found some parallels to the laws of Israel in the laws of other peoples of the ancient Near East, for example, in the Code of Hammurabi. Yet, even there, the parallels are not exact, and the Ten Commandments, for example, form a code of law unknown to other societies. Israel's laws are different from the laws of other peoples, because they are commandments given by God, and Israel is to conduct her life according to those commandments and not according to some other rules or mores or customs.

In short, Israel is not a natural people, bound together by race or soil or economics. Israel, like the Christian Church, is a "mixed multitude" (Exodus 12:38), bound together by their common redemption out of slavery and by their willing covenant with their Lord. God's acts and Israel's loyalty to him make Israel a community — a people — and apart from God they become "no people" (cf. Hosea 1:9) in which community is impossible.

That means, therefore, that the covenant people of God — Israel and the Christian Church — are not to do just what comes naturally. It is not natural to love your enemies and to pray for those who persecute you. It is not natural to deny yourself and to take up a cross. But the followers of Jesus Christ do not succumb to natural actions and wants. They follow a Lord who is greater than nature and instinct and desire.

By the same token, the covenant people of God — Israel and the Christian Church — do not do as the society around them does. In our society, the goal is to accumulate wealth and power. But the people of God know that "the meek shall inherit the earth" and that they are to lay up for themselves not treasures on earth but treasures in heaven.

The covenant people of God — Israel and the Christian Church — do not even seek after just humanitarian values and ideals, for they know that human valuation of what is "good" or "compassionate" is always distorted by human sin and self-seeking. The "good" that we construct is never good enough, because it never measures up to the height and depth and breadth of the love of God in Jesus Christ. And the values that we hold are all tinged by our valuation of ourselves before all others. Our Lord emptied himself and became a servant for our sakes. There are very few of us who are able to get rid of ourselves and to serve others alone.

It follows, therefore, that unless we live by God's will, given us in his commandments, we will always go astray. We will never inherit that abundant life that God so much wants for us. And so God guides us and protects and loves us by giving us his law, his teaching, his merciful commandments in the New Testament. He points the way to abundant life, and he says to us, "This is the way; walk in it." And he does the same thing for Israel in the Old Testament here in our story of God's words to Moses on Mount Sinai.

The fact that we are to live by God's will and not by our own or by society's ways, makes us a unique community in the world. As the book of Numbers says of Israel, the church is "a people dwelling alone, and not reckoning itself among the nations" (Numbers 22:9). Or as Exodus 19 and 1 Peter have it, we and Israel are God's "own possession," his "peculiar treasure" (KJV), his "holy nation" (Exodus 19:5; 1 Peter 2:9), which means we are set apart for God's purpose. We are his witnesses in the world, his "kingdom of priests," set apart to "declare the wonderful deeds of him who called (us) out of darkness into his marvelous light. Once we were no people but now (we) are God's people; once we had not received mercy but now (we) have received mercy" (1 Peter 2:9-10). And we will fulfill God's purpose for our lives and for our church if we follow those unique commandments that he gives to us in his love.

Ash Wednesday

Joel 2:1-2, 12-17

Sometime between 500 and 350 B.C., post-exilic Israel experienced a devastating locust plague, followed by a drought. That experience is described in Joel chapter 1. And certainly the people suffered under the dreadful effects of those disasters. But the message of the prophet Joel — prompted not by the natural disasters, but given him as a revelation from the Lord — is that the Israelites face a still more terrible disaster if they do not repent and return to their God. "The day of the Lord is coming, it is near" (2:1).

The Day of the Lord is one of the most familiar concepts found throughout the Bible. It arose in the time of the tribal federation and of the Judges, when God fought on behalf of Israel against their enemies. Because the Lord defeated Israel's foes in those days, the idea arose that he would always be on their side, and that there would come a day — a Day of the Lord — when God would defeat all of Israel's enemies and she would be exalted among the nations.

Beginning with Amos in the eighth century B.C., the prophets turned that popular confidence upside down. Yes, the Day of the Lord is coming, they announced, the Day of God's final judgment, when he would defeat all of his enemies and bring in his kingdom on earth. But far from being exalted, sinful Israel too would be judged. "Woe to you who desire the Day of the Lord!" Amos proclaimed. "Why do you desire the Day of the Lord? It is darkness and not light" (Amos 5:18).

Many of the prophets who came after Amos affirmed that dreadful message, as does Joel here in 2:1-2 (cf. Zephaniah 1; Isaiah 2:6-22; Ezekiel 7; Malachi 4:5; 3:1-5). Sinful Israel is not going to get off scot free with her sins against God, but rather will be judged like all the peoples. The darkness and gloom of the Day is near, and there is, spread upon the mountains, the awful judging hosts of

God's armies (2:2), of God's "foe from the north," as Jeremiah calls them (Jeremiah 4-6). Chapter 3 of Joel vividly pictures the judgment taking place on the Day, and Joel 2:28-32 portrays the events that will precede it.

The thought of the last judgment on the Day of the Lord continues into the New Testament. "We shall all stand before the judgment seat of God," writes Paul (Romans 14:10), and throughout the New Testament, the Day of the Lord is consistently connected with Christ's second coming, with his final judgment of us, and with his establishment of the Kingdom of God on earth. Thus, Paul's constant prayer is that his churches will be found guiltless and blameless on the Day of the Lord and thus be able to stand and inherit eternal life in the judgment (cf. the epistle lessons for Ash Wednesday: Romans 13:11-13; 1 Corinthians 1:8; 1 Thessalonians 3:13).

Our indifferent and corrupt society does not believe that God judges anyone, of course. The little godlet that we have fashioned for ourselves in our naivete is only kind and benevolent, ready to help us out of a jam, but never accusing and judgmental, always willing to forgive, no matter what our attitude toward him. But the God of the Old and New Testaments is the Lord, and his lordship cannot be mocked. What we have sown, we shall also reap, writes Paul (Galatians 6:7), just as our Lord portrays all peoples called to account for their actions before the judgment seat of the Son of Man (Matthew 25:31-46). We, who have been made in the image of God, are responsible to him, and his question to us will be, "What is this you have done?" (Genesis 3:13). Thus, on this Ash Wednesday, in some churches our foreheads are marked with ashes from the Palm Sunday celebration of the Christ whom we have crucified, and we are told, "Remember that you are dust," (cf. Genesis 3:19), just as Paul reminds us that "the wages of sin is death" (Romans 6:21).

That is not the end of the story, however, for our lesson in Joel continues, and there is spoken into our sinful lives God's little word "yet." "Nevertheless." "But." God brings a counter message, an announcement of good news (2:12-13). "Even now," God says through his prophet, you can return to me and be forgiven. Now,

76

on this day, in the midst of our situation, when our sins have multiplied and we have been heedless of our God. Even now when not one of us has the goodness to stand in the judgment of our Lord, and not one of us measures up to what God intended us to be. Even now, when our weakness, our pride, our selfishness, and our terribly human mistakes have earned for us nothing but the censure of our Lord, we can nevertheless know his forgiveness and be restored to fellowship with him, to give us the certain hope of eternal life in his kingdom.

We are called to repentance on this Ash Wednesday, and that repentance involves, says our Joel text, a rending of our hearts (v. 13). For it is in our hearts that our sin lies, is it not? In our inner beings, where we nurse our grudges and hatreds, where our desires and lusts lie, where we fashion our self-will, heedless of the will of God. What comes out of a person, Jesus teaches, is what defiles him or her — "evil thoughts, fornication, theft, murder, adultery, coveting, wickedness, deceit, licentiousness, envy, slander, pride, foolishness" — thus does our Lord catalogue our sins (Mark 7:20-23). And so it is in our hearts that we need to repent of our waywardness and to direct our lives toward our God. Outward show of fasting in Lent, evident acts of piety are not enough. God wants our inner turning with all our heart.

We should not be misled, however. It is not because we clean up our lives that God forgives us. Rather, our text says that it is because the Lord "is gracious and merciful, slow to anger, and abounding in steadfast love" (2:13). We can never coerce God's love for us by something we do. But in contrast to our hearts, God's is a heart of pure love, finally revealed to us in the cross of Jesus Christ. There on Golgotha, he pours out his forgiveness, even while we are still sinners, and so the mark of ashes on our foreheads on Ash Wednesday becomes not the mark of death, but of life and love to all eternity. Yes, apart from that sacrifice of Christ on the cross, you and I will die. But Jesus Christ also rose from the dead and now lives and loves us. And his goodness is sufficient to forgive us in the eyes of our God and to give us his eternal life. Indeed, his Spirit living in us is able to make us new persons in God's sight.

77

So it all comes down to trusting God's love in our Lord Jesus Christ, you see, repenting of our sin in the depths of our hearts, and giving them fully to our Lord, that he may remake us into the persons that he wants us to be and that we may inherit eternal life in his good kingdom that is coming. Surely, the love of Christ now demands from us our love, our life, our all.

First Sunday in Lent

Genesis 2:15-17; 3:1-7

The first thing we should realize about our texts from Genesis is that they are intended as depictions of our life with God. The Hebrew word for "Adam" means "humankind," and the writer of Genesis 2-3 is telling us that this is our story, that this is the way we all have walked with our Lord.

Thus we learn from Genesis 2 that while we were created in the most intimate fashion by God and given his breath of life that fills our lungs in their regular pumping (v. 7), God nevertheless set limits on our existence. And those limits are symbolized by that tree of the knowledge of good and evil in the garden that God planted for Adam (vv. 8, 16, 17). The fact that God forbids us to eat of that tree does not mean that he forbids us to pursue scientific knowledge or even to go to the moon. Rather, the tree stands for the fact that we are not gods and goddesses, that we cannot construct our own right and wrong, that we cannot run our own lives and plan our own futures, but rather that we are dependent on God for knowing good and evil and for our ultimate destiny. We are not the masters of our own fate and the captains of our own souls, no matter how much our society would like us to be autonomous, self-governing individuals. No. We are creatures, wondrously fashioned in love by our Creator, and dependent on him for the continuance and direction and goal of our living. And if we try to live apart from that dependence, God tells us, we will surely die (v. 17).

The story of us all that we find in 3:1-7, then, is the portrayal of our attempts to shake our relationship and dependence on our Creator — in short, to run our own lives and to be our own deities.

The serpent in these verses is not intended to be the figure of Satan. He has been created by the Lord, and his only distinguishing characteristic is that he is more subtle than any other wild creature that the Lord God has made (v. 1). He actually is just a character that the writer of this tenth century B.C. text uses to tell the story of all human beings.

The serpent engages the woman in what Dietrich Bonhoeffer has called the first conversation *about* God. That is, the serpent leads the woman to step outside of her intimate relation with her Maker and to discuss God as an object — always a disastrous step. And what the serpent does in that conversation is to set three temptations before the woman.

First, the serpent tempts the woman to think that God is not good (v. 1), that he won't give the woman what she desires and what will be good for her (cf. v. 6). But like all of us pious folk, the woman is very zealous to defend God, and so she replies that she and her husband may eat of any tree except that in the midst of the garden, "Neither shall you touch it, lest you die" (v. 3). The Lord never said not to touch the tree, of course. And so a little self-will has entered the picture. The woman has begun setting up her own tiny rules. The door is open just a crack, and the serpent sees his opportunity.

The serpent therefore tempts the woman to believe that God is not serious. "You will not die" (v. 4). God is not really serious about his commandments — all of those instructions that he has given us in his love. You shall not kill, or commit adultery; you shall not steal or bear false witness; you shall not covet. "Love your neighbor as yourself." "Take up your cross and follow me." Nah. God is not serious about all those commandments. We won't suffer any punishment or evil circumstances if we ignore what God has said. His threat is just a bunch of bluff.

The third temptation, then, is to believe that God is jealous, that he cannot stand to have someone challenge his authority and status. "God knows that when you eat of it your eyes will be opened and you will be like God, knowing good and evil" (v. 5).

There follow, therefore, two telling accounts of our sin against God, in verse 6. The woman sees that the fruit is good for food, and that it is a delight to the eyes, and that it is desired to make one wise. In other words, eating the fruit looks like the right thing to do at the time! And that is the way it is with our sin, isn't it? It looks like the right thing to do! There are very few of us who set out deliberately to do something wrong — at least not very often. We want to be good people. We want to live Christian lives. And some action looks like the good and right thing to do in some situation. It looks like the "loving" thing to do, like the "compassionate" act to take. And so we do what we think is proper. The only difficulty is that it goes against the command of God, as Eve's action goes against God's specific Word. And so we fall into sin, trying to do the "right thing" by following our own desires or wisdom.

But Adam's action in this story is typical of our sinfulness too. "And she gave to her husband, and he ate." In other words, he just goes along, as we just go along and fall into the sin of complicity. Someone makes a racial slur, and we just stand there and don't say a word. We just go along.

The result of our failure to heed God's commandments and to follow his will for our lives results in the distortion and corruption of every one of the good gifts that God has given us in his good creation. And that is illustrated by verse 7 of our text. The man and the woman in this story, who stand for you and me, were created as mutual helpers for one another, to be joined together in the joyful oneness of matrimonial love (3:18, 23-25). But when they break God's commandments and try to go it on their own and to be their own god and goddess, that good gift of marital one flesh is disrupted (v. 7). Suddenly there is a split between them, and the man's ego stands over against the woman's ego, and they are ashamed in their nakedness. And that mirrors the terrible battle and disharmony of the sexes that we know so well in our culture.

But what a pathetic ending is given to our text (v. 7). This man and woman — you and me — have wanted to be their own masters of their lives, shaping their own course, and deciding on their own what are right and wrong. They have wanted to be glorious creatures, replacing the glorious God and making him unnecessary. Instead, they must sew fig leaves together to hide their own nakedness from one another. There we are, in all of our glory and misery, wanting to be like God, and turning out to be pathetic and unclothed trespassers instead. It is a telling portrayal of our lives as sinful human beings.

Second Sunday in Lent

Genesis 12:1-4a

In order to understand this scripture lesson, it is of utmost importance that we put it in its context. Last Sunday we heard the story of Adam and Eve in the Garden of Eden, where they tried to shake off their dependence and relationship with God and to become their own deities and masters of their own lives. That attempt was symbolized by their eating of the fruit of the tree of the knowledge of good and evil in the midst of the garden. And you remember that we said that story was the symbol of the way we all have walked with our God. We all have tried to make God unnecessary and to be our own gods and goddesses.

The stories that follow the account of Adam and Eve in Genesis 3-11, then portray the spread of our sin among all humankind and God's increasingly severe judgment on that wrong. In the story of Cain and Abel, brother is set against brother, and Cain slays Abel. The result is that Cain becomes a fugitive and a wanderer on the face of the earth, cut off from all community (Genesis 4:1-14), and Cain is intended as the symbol of the hatred and dissension within our families. The sin spreads farther until we get the account of Lamech's terrible sword of vengeance, in Genesis 4:23-24, and he is the symbol of our violence and warfare that we wreak throughout the earth. That results in the story of the flood in the time of Noah, when God sees that "every imagination of the thoughts of (our) hearts is only evil continually" and so is sorry that he has made us on this earth (Genesis 6:5-6). God therefore destroys his creation with the waters of the flood, and yet human beings do not improve. The final story in Genesis 11, therefore, is the story of the Tower of Babel, when we human beings set out to storm the heights of heaven and to make a name for ourselves, in order to guarantee that we will have fame and security. But that attempt to prosper and save our own lives is thwarted by God's judgment on our sinful self-seeking. He confuses our language and scatters us abroad on the face of the earth (Genesis 11:7-9).

What is the state of human society because of our rebellion against God, therefore, according to this primeval history in the first eleven chapters of Genesis — that account that is the story of us all? We could read of it in our morning newspapers. We have corrupted all of God's good gifts — his gift of family and love, his good gifts of beauty and work, his gift of community among neighbors and nations, and yes, his gift of fellowship with himself. We are cut off from our God and from each other and from the natural world by our sin. We have passed the point of no return and have lost our paradise (cf. Genesis 3:22-24). And so we have brought upon ourselves the judgment of death, for "the wages of sin is death" (Romans 6:23).

To be sure, at every point in the story in Genesis 3-11, God's grace follows his judgment. Adam and Eve do not immediately die. They are clothed by God himself — God the tailor — and God helps Eve have a child (Genesis 3:21; 4:1). Despite the fact that Cain is driven away from the face of God and from every human community (Genesis 4:14), the Lord nevertheless puts a mark on him, so no one will kill him (4:15). In the flood, Noah and his family and representatives of every living creature are saved on the ark (6:18-19), and God himself makes sure that the door of the ark is tightly sealed (7:16). And following the flood, an even fuller life is given to humankind with the rainbow promise that never again will the Lord destroy his creation by the chaotic waters (8:20—9:17).

Yet, we have to ask: Where is the grace at the end of the story of the Tower of Babel? Is Babel God's last word? Are we all doomed forever to have no love or peace or sense of community among neighbors and nations, between brothers and sisters, between husbands and wives? Are we all left with the beauty of the earth turned to thorns and thistles by our ravaging, and God's good gift of work turned into drudgery and futility (3:17-19)? Are we all cut off from our God forever and therefore fated to die, apart from him who is the one source of all life and good?

84

The answers to those questions are furnished by our text for the morning. God calls one man named Abraham out of his home in Mesopotamia, in about 1750 B.C., and he tells Abraham to leave behind his country, his kinfolk, and his closest relatives, and to journey to an unknown land that God will show to Abraham (12:1). At the same time, God gives Abraham a threefold promise. He will give a land to Abraham and his descendants that they may call their own (cf. 12:7). He will make of Abraham's descendants a great nation and make their name renowned (12:2). And through Abraham and his descendants, God will bring blessing on all the families of the earth (12:3).

Those promises pick up motifs from chapter 11. At the Tower of Babel, humankind has tried to make a name for itself (11:4), but it is God who will make Israel's name great (12:2). In 11:30, we read that Sarai, the wife of Abraham, is barren and has no child. But God promises Abraham that his descendants will be numerous enough to make a large nation (12:2). Thus does the Lord contradict the sinful course of our lives and history.

At the same time, God's promise to father Abraham is a vow to reverse the effects of our cursed rebellion that was portrayed for us in Genesis 3-11. We lost our paradise, said that primeval history, so God sets out to give Abraham and his people a new land "flowing with milk and honey." We made all community impossible, so the Lord will make a new community, a great nation called Israel. And the Old Testament later tells us that God's intention is to draw all peoples into that new fellowship (cf. e.g. Isaiah 2:2-4; 44:5; Zechariah 8:20-23; Ephesians 2:12-22). We brought upon ourselves the curse of devastation and drudgery and death. God promises to turn it all into blessing through his instrument of Abraham and his people.

In short, God calls Abraham because he loves us all, and is determined to overcome the effects of our sin in our lives and in our world. God sets out in the father of our faith to restore us all to the good life that he intended for us all in the beginning. There is therefore added to this threefold promise in Genesis 12 also the promise of a covenant with Israel, in which humankind's relation with God will be restored (Genesis 17:4-7). And when Jesus Christ

85

sat at table at the Lord's Supper and offered us the new covenant in his blood, that promise was fulfilled (Mark 14:24).

That is what God is doing here and now in our world, good Christians. He is working to keep his word, to reverse the effects of our sin, to bring blessing on us all, to make of us a new people, living in a new community of peace and beauty, meaningful work and goodness, fullness of life (which is what "blessing" means) and love. And the story of how God works to keep his promises is the story that runs through the entire Bible.

If we believe that sacred history and make it ours, by trusting our God, we will be blessed, as our text for the morning says. For God tells Abraham, "I will bless those who bless you, and him who curses you, I will curse" (Genesis 12:3). Our life or death, it seems, depends on our attitude toward God's promise and working, begun with Abraham. And if, in faith, we will accept God's words and his actions within our lives, we shall indeed know fullness of life.

Third Sunday in Lent

Exodus 17:1-7

Israel is underway in this story, as the church is underway. Israel's story is our story. She has been redeemed out of slavery in Egypt, just as we have been redeemed by the cross and resurrection of Jesus Christ out of our slavery to sin and death. And now, like Israel, you and I are making our way through the wilderness toward a promised land of rest. We are midway between our redemption and our final salvation in the Kingdom of God. The goal toward which we press lies out there ahead of us (cf. Philippians 3:12), as the promise land lay out ahead of Israel.

But as we journey on this pilgrimage of ours toward our final salvation, surely we, like Israel, find ourselves in a desolate and forbidding wilderness. Israel was threatened by heat and thirst, hunger and scorpions and jackals. We, in our comfortable lifestyle, know none of those things. But we do know fear of illness and death, don't we — fear of disrupted loves and disappointments in relationships; fear of violence and terrorists, of crime and sudden calamities, of a world that has lost all sense of good and that is plunging into chaos. And in the midst of our own private and corporate wildernesses, we are like the Israelites. We look for someone to blame.

It is notable in our text that Israel, despite all of the wonders of the exodus that she has experienced from God's hands, directs her eyes solely to the human realm. She blames Moses for her difficulties. *He* has led her out of slavery into her trouble. *He* is blamed for her thirst and privation. His purpose is to kill the adults and children and cattle. He is at fault. Here is a people who has been delivered from the pursuing troops of the Pharaoh and led safely on dry land through the Reed Sea, not by Moses' power but by God's. Here is a folk who has been guarded at front and rear by God's protection in pillar of fire and cloud. Here is a company that has been delivered into a foretaste of "the glorious liberty of the children of God." And yet, when she faces renewed dangers, she forgets all God has done and considers her fate to be entirely in the hands of a human being.

We are very much like that, aren't we? We remain in our vision of life on a human level. Our lives, we think, are in the hands, not of God, but of the politicians, the military, the multinational corporations. Our successes and failures are due to our bosses, our spouses, or yes, to luck or chance. Maybe a teacher misguided us, or our parents didn't raise us right. Maybe we grew up in the wrong kind of environment or were at the wrong place at the wrong time. Or just maybe we ourselves have to work a little harder, or learn better how to get along, or read that new "how to" book in order to improve our lot. Our pilgrimage, we think, is a solely human journey, and God has nothing to do with it.

One of the reasons Moses is such a towering figure in the Old Testament, however, is because he knows who is in charge of all life. Moses knows that he is not leading his people. God is. And Moses knows, in the midst of difficulties, to whom to turn. He does not try to justify his leadership or to make excuses for the people's situation. No. Moses prays to God for help in his desperate situation. Moses knows that the Israelites really are questioning not him, but God's guidance. They are putting not him but God to the test.

Moses' cry to God for help is genuine. He does not know what the answer will be to his plea for aid. He himself cannot fathom why God has brought them into such a wilderness situation. He simply, in faith, turns to his Lord whom he knows is always present, because he realizes that we have to do in our wildernesses not just with human beings, but with the Lord who is always with us.

The incredible happening is that for his disobedient people, God supplies their need. If you read through the stories of Israel's wilderness wanderings, you find a continual history of complaint (cf. Exodus 15:22-25; Numbers 11:4-6; 14:1-3; 20:1-13). And yet, God, in the face of all of our complaints, our forgetfulness of him, our lack of trust, supplies his faithless people with water to quench their thirst. And that water is not provided from an unnoticed spring or succulent desert plant, but from a rock, because God is Lord over nature's ways too. He could send ten plagues upon the enslaving Egyptians and roll back the waters of the Reed Sea. So too, as the Lord of all nature and history, he can bring forth drink from stone. But Moses names the place of that supplying water Massah and Meribah, meaning "proof" and "contention," as the perpetual reminder of the fact that Israel — and we — constantly complain in all our difficulties, and never remember with what forgiving mercy we are being supplied by our God.

The final verse of our text says that Israel's question was, "Is the Lord with us or not?" But actually, through most of the story, Israel never even considers that question. She forgets entirely that it is God who is guiding her pilgrimage, despite the fact that Moses early (v. 2) tries to remind her of God's leading. And we, who repeatedly hear in our churches that God is with us and guiding us, seem always to think not of God, but solely of human matters. We remain on our profane and secular level, and never see God's working among us.

May I remind you, then, that God is guiding your individual lives and the life of this church on a pilgrimage toward his good kingdom? That he has redeemed us all out of slavery to sin and death by the sacrifice and resurrection of his Son? And that Jesus Christ has promised that he will be with us always, even to the end of time? We are not alone as we journey through all the difficulties and terrors of our wilderness existence. Jesus Christ goes with us, a front guard and a rear guard, and our Savior always in our midst. And more than that, he tells us that in our time of thirst for good and need for victory over evil and even death, his is the Spirit that can give us water welling up to eternal life (John 4:13-14). "If anyone thirst," he teaches us in John's Gospel — if any of you are arched for comfort and guidance, for strength and goodness and love — "come to me and drink," (John 7:37) our Savior says, and never thirst again.

Fourth Sunday in Lent

1 Samuel 16:1-13

This story forms the beginning of the narrative of David's rise to power that is found in 1 Samuel 16—2 Samuel 5. In that narrative, three different stories are told about how David comes to public attention. At the end of chapter 16, he becomes a member of Saul's court because he can play skillfully upon the lyre to soothe Saul's fits of depression. In chapter 17, David is celebrated as the slayer of Goliath. And in 18:5-9, David is honored by the populace as a warrior who is always successful in their battles against the threatening Philistines. It is David's anointing here in chapter 16:1-13, however, that gives the interpretive framework for all else that follows.

It is important to remember that at the time of this story, Saul is still king over Israel. Toward the end of the eleventh century B.C., Israel was literally threatened with annihilation at the hands of the Philistines, who dwelt in five city states along the coast of Palestine. The loose federation of the twelve tribes that had up to that time furnished volunteers for Israel's army was too weak to withstand the Philistine incursion. As a result, the people of Israel demanded that Samuel appoint for them a king to lead them in battle (1 Samuel 8:4-22). Samuel objected to such a request, because he knew that the Lord was the real King over Israel (1 Samuel 8:4-8) and that the people's demand was evidence of a lack of faith in the Lord's defense of his covenant folk (1 Samuel 10:17-19; 12:6-12). As a result, the kingship of Saul had a cloud of disapproval over it from the beginning — a disapproval that is found also in later prophetic writings (cf. Hosea 8:4). And the theology of human kingship in the Old Testament always stands in some tension with the Mosaic theology of the Hexateuch (cf. Deuteronomy 17:14-20).

Nevertheless, here begins in our text for the morning the initiation of that royal theology that leads eventually to the thought of a Messiah, an anointed davidic king, and to the expectation of the coming of a perfectly righteous king who will guarantee the Lord's favor toward Israel (cf. Isaiah 9:1-7; 11:1-9; Jeremiah 23:5-6; Ezekiel 37:24-25).

Despite the fact that Saul is still on the throne, God has rejected him as the king over Israel (1 Samuel 16:1). The stories leading up to that rejection are found in 1 Samuel 13:1-15 and 15:1-31. Now God seeks a shepherd-king for his people who is a man after his heart. Now God himself accepts the kingship as necessary to his people's existence.

The kingship of the Lord remains prominent in the story, however, for only he can decide who should rule Israel. Indeed, Samuel must explicitly follow the Lord's instructions in order to identify that ruler. Samuel must go to Bethlehem (later known as the "city of David," Luke 2:4), taking with him a sacrifice.

Bethlehem is in the southern region of Palestine, outside of Saul's circle of influence, and it is a risky trip — a flaunting of Saul's authority. Anyone as important as Samuel is obviously not making the journey just to offer a sacrifice; Samuel is plotting treason against Saul. And so Jesse and his family nervously receive Samuel and go along with his deception. They ritually prepare themselves and accompany Samuel to the place of offering.

The scene that follows deliberately builds suspense for the reader. One by one Jesse calls his seven sons to pass in front of Samuel. The first son, Eliab, is so handsome that Samuel thinks surely he must be the chosen one. But God tells Samuel to judge, not by outward appearance, but by the heart and character of the man. So the next six do not pass the test. Is there then no one left? Well, there is an eighth young son who is out tending the sheep. A messenger is sent to fetch the as-yet-unnamed youth, while they all wait for the young man's appearance. Finally, he arrives and the Lord tells Samuel that the young shepherd is the chosen one. Samuel therefore follows the Lord's instructions and anoints the chosen future king. Only then are we finally told that his name is David.

Two classes of persons were anointed in Israel — priests and kings — and the anointing with oil was the outward symbol of the gift of the Spirit, just as our baptism with water is a similar outward symbol of the receipt of the Spirit. Our text says therefore that "the Spirit of the Lord came mightily upon David from that day forward" (v. 13). Just as with baptism, that sacramental act is entirely the Lord's doing. David has not deserved the gift or done anything to receive it. Rather he is the recipient of the objective act of God.

It is strange in our text that despite verse 7, the outward appearance of David is described in verse 12 — surely an indication of the narrator's and the people's subsequent love for David. He was so fair to look at, they remember! And yet what mixed blessings awaited him, according to the stories that follow in the Samuel books!

The point of the narrative for us, however, is very clear. God's choice of persons and events is the determining factor of human history. We may think that God has little hand in the round of our daily lives and world. We may think that all of our fortunes and misfortunes stem from our own efforts and actions. But this story, and indeed all of the biblical stories, give the lie to such thoughts. God is the real Ruler. He chooses and establishes leaders, or he brings them to disgrace and fall (cf. Isaiah 40:23-24; Jeremiah 1:10). He searches the hearts of individuals and blesses them or curses (cf. Psalm 139:23; Jeremiah 17:10). Indeed, human history is one great dialogue between God and human beings, in which God speaks and acts, and human beings react accordingly. And then God in turns shapes events and motives nevertheless to further his good purpose.

God desired, in 1000 B.C., to anoint a son of Jesse, to begin that line of davidic kings — that line of *mashiachs* or messiahs — that would, in the fullness of time, find its final representative in Jesus of Nazareth, born in Bethlehem of Judea and yet Son of God, and anointed forever by the Spirit of God to redeem and save the world. God's plan of salvation stretches over centuries of time. But at the end of it lies the goal of the Kingdom of God — our true Ruler — come on earth. You and I stand in that ongoing history, and we can further it or oppose it. But God is the Lord, and his purpose will be fulfilled.

Fifth Sunday in Lent

Ezekiel 37:1-14

This famous vision of the Valley of Dry Bones is given to the prophet Ezekiel in Babylonia shortly after the fall of Jerusalem to Babylonia in 587 B.C. As in 1:3 and 8:1, the prophet is seized "by the hand of the Lord," that is, he is sent into an ecstatic state in which he is given to see new reality.

Israel considers itself to be dead in exile (cf. 33:10; Isaiah 53:8-9). She has lost her land, her temple, her davidic king, her covenant, and her relationship with her God. The forces of death have overwhelmed her, and now her exiles are without the possibility of life, like long-dry bones, scattered aimlessly about a parched and desolate valley. No human help can restore her. She is beyond all hope.

Ezekiel therefore hears the enigmatic question asked him by God, "Son of man, can these bones live?" (v. 3). It is a question that can confront us, too, can it not? When life crumbles in on us and loving relationships are gone; when pain accompanies our every hour and makes normality impossible; when anxieties haunt our nights and days and undermine every security; when evil stalks our city streets and we can trust no stranger; when our world seems bathed in nothing but bloody violence and all goodness seems to be impossible; we too wonder if there can ever be possibility of whole life again. And we feel our hope dried up and our future as nothing but ominous.

Our prophet wisely answers the question from God about the dry bones. Can these bones live? "O Lord God, thou knowest." Human means are not sufficient to overwhelm the forces of death that hold captive our life and world. Try as we may, we seem never able to set all things right. Broken relationships, suffering, crime, violence, and evil — none of our programs seem to do away with them forever. For every solution, there is a new problem, for every program, an unforeseen shortcoming, and unless healing and restoration are in the hands of God, good life seems impossible. Our bones are dried up; we are clean cut off. O God, will you restore us?

It is unfortunate that this text from Ezekiel has been paired in the lectionary with the gospel lesson in John 11. For that passage talks about the final resurrection of the dead. But this passage from Ezekiel is not looking to bodily resurrection after death. It is talking about the restoration and healing of our life here and now. And it is saying that only God can work that transformation.

Ezekiel therefore is bidden by the Lord to prophesy, to speak the powerful, life-giving Word of God. And as he does so, he is given the vision of the dry bones come together in ordered skeletons. Then there come on the bones sinews and flesh and skin, and they have bodily form. But they as yet have no life in them. They are still the inert dead (vv. 7-8).

The prophet must therefore speak the Word of God once more, summoning from the four winds the breath of life. And as that breath enters the inert forms, they live, and they stand upon their feet, "an exceedingly great host" (vv. 9-10).

In short, the breath that animates the persons in the vision is not to be understood as the Spirit of God. Rather, it is that breath of life, like the first breath of God breathed into Adam at his creation (Genesis 2:7), and like that breath by which God sustains all living creatures alive (Psalm 104:29). Life, our text is saying, is sustained only by the faithfulness of God, for were the Creator to hold his breath, we would return to dead physical matter. We have our life in God, whether we know it or not.

In the last portion of our text, verses 11-14, the Lord interprets the vision for his prophet. Israel has been dead in exile. But like bodies being exhumed from the grave, Israel will be raised up once more by her Lord and returned to her homeland, where she will be granted life and a future and a hope anew (cf. Jeremiah 29:10-11). Israel is not "clean cut off," as she has believed (v. 11). She is not destined simply to wither away and die in a foreign land. God has not deserted her (cf. Isaiah 40:27). Rather, he treasures her as the "apple of his eye" (Deuteronomy 32:10) and loves her and will

restore her to a good life. And so there are found in Ezekiel's prophecies, after God's judgments, the promises of a loving God for the
good future of his beloved people.

Well, can your bones live? In whatever desperate or insolvable
situation you find yourself, do you feel that you are "clean cut off"
from your God and that there is no hope for your future except that
dreary stereotype of "one damn thing after another"? Have you no
hope for anything better, no expectation of good ahead of you?

Speaking of each of us personally, surely some of us are as
good as dead spiritually, cut off from all consciousness of anything
beyond ourselves. And we're just living out nine-to-five in what
have been called "lives of quiet desperation." What we see is all
we get and any thought of a spiritual realm or of anything having
to do with God is far from our minds and hearts.

Similarly, some among us are as good as dead morally, and we
have abandoned all definitions of right and wrong. If it feels good,
we do it, don't we? And then we wonder why we feel an unease
about the way we are conducting our lives or why there is such
chaos in the society that we help mold.

If that is your condition on this fifth Sunday in Lent, or on any
other, the words of Ezekiel can give us life too. For he tells us that
by the Word of the Lord, we can be transformed — that we who
feel ourselves lost and dead can find ourselves alive again — alive
and whole by the powerful Word of God who is Jesus Christ. Can
your bones live again? Yes, in Christ your Lord, who came that
you might have life and have it more abundantly.

As for our hopeless, violent, death-dealing world, the Word of
God who is our Lord Christ will transform that also. And he promises that beyond the valley of death in which all peoples seem to be
captive these days, there is a shining realm of good that is known
as the Kingdom of God, where death shall be no more, and sorrow
and sighing and pain will have passed away. His kingdom comes,
good Christians. Dry bones will live again. And God will be all in
all, to all eternity.

Passion/Palm Sunday

Isaiah 50:4-9a

As we approach the story of our Lord's suffering during what we call this Holy Week, and especially as we draw near to the remembrance of his crucifixion on Friday, we search the scriptures for clues to the interpretation of his passion — for guides to understand the deepest meaning of all that Jesus goes through. And surely, few passages in the Old Testament help us more to understand than do the four Servant Songs that are found in what we call the Second Isaiah book.

Most scholars now agree that Isaiah is to be divided into three distinct books, all of which share common motifs and theology, but which were assembled in three different periods in Israel's life: Isaiah chapters 1-39 from about 740 B.C.; Isaiah 40-55 from 550-538 B.C. and addressed to Israel exiled in Babylonia; and Isaiah 56-66 from various times after 538 B.C. to Israelites returned to Jerusalem. Our text for the morning forms the third Servant Song in Second Isaiah, the others being Isaiah 42:1-4; 49:1-6; and the famous Suffering Servant Song in Isaiah 52:13—53:12, which we will treat in two weeks.

Probably the Servant in this song is to be identified with an idealized Israel of the future (cf. Isaiah 41:8-9; 42:19; 43:10; 44:1-2, 21; 45:4; 48:20) — Israel as she is meant to be, Israel as Second Isaiah calls her to be. As that Servant, Israel is called by her God in 50:4-9a to suffer for the sake of all nations — a call particularly clear in 52:13—53:12 and in the passion of our Lord. But surely, this passage in 50:4-9a also reflects the nature of the office of all true prophets and the nature of Second Isaiah's prophetic ministry itself.

The prophet tells us the source of all true prophecy in the Old Testament. It comes from God. The prophet is like a pupil before a schoolmaster God, and God alone gives him the words he is to speak. Every morning God wakens the prophet's ear and delivers to him the words he is to proclaim (v. 4). Apart from that communication from God, the prophet has nothing to say. Only false prophets give their own opinions or pontificate on the course of events out of their own minds (cf. Jeremiah 23:18-32; Ezekiel 13:6-7). They are like those preachers who preach out of their own thoughts and not out of the Word of God given in the scriptures.

This intimate teaching given by God to his servants shows us that we really cannot understand the prophetic writings except in a similar intimate relation with our God, namely, in day-by-day prayer and meditation with him. True prophecy rises out of the closest fellowship with the Lord, and we can understand it also only in that context.

Our text tells us, however, that the prophet-servant of the Lord is attacked and abused because of the message that he delivers (vv. 5-6). He is whipped, taunted by having his beard pulled out, spit upon, and scorned by his contemporaries. In short, he becomes a laughing-stock, as did the prophet Jeremiah also (Jeremiah 20:1-3). The populace neither believes nor heeds his message. And the servant knows that will be his fate! Yet, he does not shrink from his task, given him by God (v. 5). He sets his face "like a flint" (cf. the Greek of Luke 9:51) to proclaim God's Word and to suffer the consequences.

Whence comes the servant's confidence in the face of calumny? It comes from God, who "helps" him (v. 7). He will finally be shamed in his society only if his prophecy proves untrue. But in his intimate relation to God, he knows that he "shall not be put to shame" (v. 7). God will prove his Word true; God will, by his actions toward Israel, fulfill the words that the prophet-servant speaks. The servant will be shown to be right — vindicated (v. 8). And of course that demonstration is why we have particular prophecies in the Old Testament — because they proved true in history and were fulfilled and brought to pass and therefore shown to be the true words of God.

In such confidence, the prophet-servant issues a challenge to his abusers. "Who will contend with me?" he asks (v. 8). That is, who will go to court with me? Let him state his case. Because God, who helps the prophet, will prove him innocent of falsehood, while those who have opposed the prophet will meet their end.

That the portrayal given us in this passage accurately describes what happens to our Lord in the last week his life cannot be doubted — although this is not a prediction in the Old Testament of the Christ. Rather, it is a description of the true prophet and servant's role, and Jesus Christ takes upon himself and fulfills the final shape of that role during the week of his passion. Our Lord speaks and does only what he hears from God (cf. John 8:28). He willingly accepts the suffering that comes with that ministry. "Not my will, but thine be done" (Mark 14:36 KJV). He is subjected to scorn and whipping and spitting, like the servant before him (Mark 15:15-20). And finally he is killed for his faithfulness to his God. But God does not desert his servants, not even in death, and so there will come Easter morn when all that Jesus Christ has said and done will be vindicated and proved true. His will be shown to be the way that leads to eternal life. His will be shown to be the true will of God.

If we can bring our text down to a personal level for a moment, is this not a message for all of us servants of God, also? It is not easy to be a follower of Jesus Christ in our age and society. There are some in our world who are suffering torture and death for that faithfulness. But even in our country, we may be laughed at, shunned, denied opportunities because of our faith. And we may have to suffer to hold a marriage together, or eschew some material comforts, or stand up to criticism and scorn for our way of life (cf. 1 Peter 4:1-6). After all, our Lord proclaimed that those of us who would be his disciples are required to take up a cross and die to our own wills and desires.

But if this Servant Song and the passion of our Lord teach us nothing else, they witness to the fact that God's way, taught us in the scriptures, is true — that it is the way that leads to life and to joy eternal. God never deserts his servants. And he will vindicate his own. As Paul writes, "If God is for us, who is against us?" (Romans 8:31). Nothing and no one can defeat us. And in the end, we shall be even more than conquerors through him who loves us (Romans 8:37).

Maundy/Holy Thursday

Exodus 12:1-4 (5-10), 11-14

The Gospels tell us that on the night that he was betrayed, our Lord first celebrated the Passover with his disciples. Thus it is important for us to go back in Exodus to the founding of the Passover celebration and its meaning.

There have been numerous scholarly speculations about the origin of Passover. Some have thought it was originally a semi-nomadic spring celebration that petitioned the deity's favor and protection during the migration of flocks from one pasture to another. Others have connected it with ancient Near Eastern New Year festivals. However that may be, the scriptures are clear about the origins of the festival for Israel. It formed the prelude and preparation for Israel's deliverance out of slavery in Egypt in the thirteenth century B.C.

God was about to redeem his enslaved people, to set them free from their bondage, to form them into a community and adopt them as his son (cf. Hosea 11:1), and to deliver them into the beginning of "the glorious liberty of the children of God," pointed toward a promised land to call their own. Exodus 12 gives us the liturgical preparation and explanation (vv. 21-23) for that saving exodus event. It is the prelude to God's "redemption," which signifies "buying back" out of slavery (cf. Leviticus 25:47-49).

Each Israelite family was to roast a lamb of goat or sheep on the evening of the fourteenth day of the month of Abib (March-April). Passover was and is always a family affair, or if the family was poor, it was to be shared with a neighbor. The lamb was to be without blemish (cf. John 19:36), a year old, and eaten with bitter herbs and unleavened bread. Some of the blood of the lamb was to be daubed on the doorposts and lintels of the house. If any of the meat was left, it was to be burned in the morning. But this first Passover was not a leisurely feast. It was to be eaten hastily, with the Israelites prepared for flight, for on the next day, the Lord would "pass over" the houses marked with blood to execute his wrath on the enslaving Egyptians and to set Israel free from her bondage.

Thus from the time of Moses on, Israel has celebrated the Passover in commemoration of the Lord's act of redeeming her out of slavery in Egypt. While originally the Passover in Exodus 12 looked forward to that redemption, in the years following, Israel's celebration looked back to the deliverance from bondage.

The exodus that Passover celebrates is the central redemptive act of God in the Old Testament, an act that is recalled in most of the Old Testament's books. It forms the supreme revelation for the chosen people of God's mercy toward the helpless (cf. Exodus 3:7-8), of his love for the folk he has adopted as his own, and of his power over empire, other gods (cf. Exodus 12:12), and nature. It is no accident, therefore, that the exodus in the Old Testament forms the parallel to the crucifixion of our Lord in the New Testament. Indeed, when Jesus talks about his death in Luke 9:31, he speaks of it as his "exodus" (in the Greek; RSV translates "departure"). Jesus' death on the cross brings our "redemption," our deliverance from slavery to sin and death. It manifests God's mercy toward all of us who are helpless in our captivity to our sin. It is the supreme manifestation of God's love (cf. Romans 5:8). And in the resurrection that follows, God's power over empire and evil and nature is manifested.

It is entirely fitting, therefore, that at this Maundy Thursday celebration of the Lord's Supper, we read the accounts of the Passover in the Old Testament and New, for the Lord's Supper remembers the crucifixion of our Lord Jesus Christ. "We do show forth his death until he comes." We remember that we too have been redeemed from our slavery to sin and death, as Israel was redeemed from her slavery in Egypt. And at this supper, we are bound together with all the faithful, past, present, and future, as the one united people of God.

This supper that we celebrate is not merely a remembrance of things past, however. When Israel celebrates the Passover in the centuries after Moses up to the present day, she not only looks back to a past event. Rather, the past becomes her present. That is the function of such liturgy. It makes events that have happened in the past the events that are happening in the present. Every individual and family finds itself redeemed from slavery in the present. The Lord "spared *our* houses," the Israelite father can say to his son (v. 27). "The Lord heard *our* voice, and saw *our* affliction, *our* toil and *our* oppression; and the Lord brought *us* out of Egypt with a mighty hand ..." (Deuteronomy 26:7-8). We are there. We are redeemed this day. We are delivered.

So it is, too, at the Lord's Supper that we celebrate now, is it not? We are there, sitting at table with our Lord on the night that one of us will betray him. He washes our feet (John's account) and bids us be servants to one another. He gives us the bread and the cup of the new covenant in his blood (1 Corinthians 11:23-26; the Synoptic Gospels). And we are redeemed and set free once again from our slavery to sin and death and reaffirmed as the beloved children of our God. The past to which we look back becomes our present in which we are set free to enjoy once more a foretaste and promise of "the glorious liberty of the children of God" (Romans 8:21). It is like the Negro spiritual says, good Christians, "Were you there when they crucified my Lord?" Oh, yes, indeed, we were there. And "sometimes it causes me to tremble." But this supper, here, now, means that we are redeemed from our sin.

In our Old Testament lesson, Moses explains aforetime what will happen on the night of Israel's redemption. The liturgy precedes the event. So too in the Gospel according to John, Jesus is the host at the supper, explaining to his disciples ahead of time what is going to happen when he is crucified and raised from the dead.

But here, now, for us, the event has taken place, hasn't it? The cross has been raised. Explanation and event are joined. As we read of the Supper and participate in it, all the power and mercy and love of God are poured out upon us. And you and I are delivered from our slaveries, and we can go out from this place a new people, a redeemed people, God's own beloved community.

Good Friday

Isaiah 52:13 — 53:12

For centuries, the Christian Church has regarded this fourth Servant Song in Second Isaiah as a prophecy that foretells the life, suffering, death, and resurrection of Jesus Christ. Certainly the New Testament uses portions of it in connection with our Lord (cf. John 12:38; Acts 8:32-33; 1 Peter 2:24-25, et al.). And yet a great air of mystery surrounds this passage. Who finally is the servant? Why has he been the object of shame and suffering all of his life? Why was he judged and killed? How did others come to recognize that he was serving God's merciful purposes? How was he exalted over death? The poem itself does not spell out the detailed answers to all of those questions. Indeed, there are even lines in the poem that defy certain translation, as scholars have long recognized. And certainly the prophet whom we call Second Isaiah had no knowledge of the incarnation of the Son of God in Jesus of Nazareth.

Rather, the prophet simply faithfully proclaimed the words that God gave him, writing them down in the sixth century B.C. for the Israelite exiles in Babylonia. And then the poem's final interpretation waited for centuries, hidden in the secret heart of God, until it was the will of God to shine the dazzling light of revelation upon it and to embody it in the person of Jesus Christ. Ever since our Lord walked this earth, this passage has helped us understand Jesus Christ, and he in turn has helped us understand this passage. So if we want to know our Lord and the meaning of his history, then this Suffering Servant Song can help us to attain that knowledge.

The text begins with God speaking in verses 13-15 of chapter 52. God announces that his servant, who was so disfigured by suffering that persons could not bear to look at him, and who was cut off from normal human acceptance and community (v. 14), will become one honored and exalted and given all good things (v. 13). And that is totally unexpected. When we see someone horribly

107

suffering in pain or disfigured, we turn away from them and do not expect them to be changed. That is unknown in our world. But the servant's lot will gloriously be transformed, and as a result, far distant places (nations) and important persons (kings) will hear of it and be totally astonished (v. 15).

In a sense, those three opening verses summarize most of the poem's thought, for in 53:1, the unknown speakers in far-off nations and exalted circles take up the speech. "Who would have believed such a transformation?" they ask (53:1). From his birth on, the servant's whole life was marred by suffering. He was weak and parched, like a plant growing up out of dry ground. He had no beauty about him, because beauty signifies blessing from God, and the servant did not seem to be blessed. No one regarded him as important (v. 2). He was a man subjected to blows and scorned, humiliated and isolated and sorrowing (v. 3).

As a result, the unknown speakers continue, we all thought he was rejected also by God. Yet, now we realize that the servant suffered because he was bearing our sins and that God was subjecting him to the punishment that should have been ours (vv. 4-6). "All we like sheep have gone astray," and the servant was atoning for our unfaithfulness to our Lord.

What causes this realization and repentance on the part of those for whom the servant suffers? Our text does not say. It simply goes on to describe the suffering that the servant undergoes for our sake. Hauled into court, the servant makes no defense of himself (v. 7). Instead he is condemned to death, and a shameful death at that. He is buried along with all the other criminals and forgotten as of no importance, even though he actually was innocent of our transgressions with which he was charged (vv. 7-9).

But all of that was God's will! God used the servant's death as the expiation for our own sin (v. 10). The innocent servant's death atoned for what all of us have done wrong! And as a result, all of us are now counted righteous in the eyes of our God (v. 11).

The servant's burial is not the end of the story, however, for God once more takes up the speech in verse 11. On the other side of the grave, beyond the finality of death, God proclaims that his

108

servant will be restored and exalted to a good and happy life (v. 11). Is that a foretelling of the resurrection of Christ? The text does not say; it gives no further details. But it is clear that the servant's humiliating death will not hold him forever, and that he will live fully as the reward for his faithful and atoning sacrifice of his life (vv. 10-12).

So it is that those events in the life of the servant, who seemed of no consequence, have all been planned and wrought by God, and that behind the suffering, the scorn, the isolation and death of the servant, there has been the unseen hand of the Lord God, working out his purpose of forgiving us all and of restoring us, despite our sin, to righteousness once again in his eyes. It is not a fanciful story, good Christians, for there are many in our world and in fact in this congregation who regard God's servant, Jesus Christ, as really of very little consequence for their daily lives. He was a man, they think, who got in trouble with the Roman and Jewish authorities of his time, and who therefore ended up dying a criminal's death on a Roman torture instrument called a cross. "So what?" is the attitude of our age. What does that have to do with me?

But somewhere along the line in our daily round perhaps God will penetrate our careless hearts and minds with the startling knowledge that Jesus Christ "was wounded for our transgressions" and "bruised for our iniquities" and "with his stripes we are healed" — healed in the eyes of our God, you see, counted righteous once more in God's sight, despite all of the sins and terribly human mistakes and weaknesses to which we all fall prey. We are forgiven, Christians, our sins atoned for by the death of our Lord. And that means that we do not have to suffer the wages of sin which is always death, and that we do not need to think that we are loosed and cut off from the hand of our God. No. Instead, through faith in the work of Jesus Christ, we can be restored to the household of our Father and know once more his loving and sustaining presence. And that is life, friends, abundant life, and joy, and eternity with our God!

Easter Day

Acts 10:34-43

The resurrection is for everyone. That is the message of our text. It tells the story of the visit of the Apostle Peter to the house of a Roman soldier named Cornelius, who is stationed with the other troops in the town of Caesarea on the northern coast of Samaria. Prompted by the vision of an angel who has urged him to summon Peter, Cornelius sends two of his servants to fetch the apostle. At the same time, Peter has been given the strange vision of a great sheet let down from heaven, filled with unclean animals, and he has been commanded by the Lord to eat what is unclean. In other words, Peter has learned that the good news of the gospel is not only for ritually pure Jews or for the faithful of Israel, but for all people everywhere. That is the realization with which Peter journeys to Cornelius' house and declares to him the content of our reading that we heard from Acts.

The resurrection of Jesus Christ is for everyone. There are some of you in this congregation who, if you will admit it honestly, are rather marginal Christians. Easter does not hold much meaning for you. It's a time when everyone buys new clothes and goes to church and thinks of Easter bunnies and colored eggs. But the resurrection has never had much significance in your daily life.

There are others who have come into this church bearing in the back of their minds the memory of a rather spotted past. What do you have on your conscience? Some compromise of what you knew was right? Some temptation and sin you placed in another's way? Some sexual or monetary misadventure that you've never been able to confess to anyone?

That is not to say, of course, that there are not also some saints among us, persons who have faithfully trusted their Lord through all of the ups and downs of their lives, persons who

111

have worshiped and prayed and studied the Bible and found their foundation in their Christian faith for years upon years.

To make the record complete, we of course must also note that outside of this church there are all of those secular souls who largely ignore whatever it is that we do in this place. Persons who live and let live, who let the church go its own way and who never give a thought to God, who figure that how they live their life is nobody's business but their own, and that whatever happens to them in this world is dependent entirely on their efforts or maybe just on luck.

So there is a whole conglomeration of people inside and outside the church on this Easter Sunday — faithful and indifferent, believing and doubting, sinners and saints. And the message of our text is that the resurrection is for all of them — for all of us, no matter what our condition. "Truly I perceive," says Peter in our text, "that God shows no partiality" (v. 34), because, you see, God so loved the *world* that he gave his only Son.

So what does that mean for all of us on this Easter morn? Most obvious I suppose is the fact that God wants to give us life. It's a foregone conclusion that all of us are going to die, isn't it? Despite all of our modern, miracle medicine, despite all of our efforts to retain our youth — by cosmetics or exercise or proper diet — sooner or later each one of us will end up in a grave. But the Lord God of the universe doesn't like death very well. In fact, the scriptures tell us that his Son is fighting a battle against it (cf. 1 Corinthians 15:25-26). God wants to do away with death. And so, as Peter tells us in our text, God sends his Son to descend into the darkness of death, but then to triumph over it. "God raised him on the third day," Peter proclaims, and there were countless witnesses to that fact (vv. 40-41). In Jesus Christ, God who hates the fact that we are going to die, triumphed over our deaths and gave us the resurrected One by whom you and I may have eternal life.

It's also true in the scriptures that God, the Lord of the universe, hates evil. The prophet Habakkuk tells us that God cannot even stand to look at it (Habakkuk 1:13). And heaven knows there's a lot he sees in our time and place, isn't there? The violence and crime on our city streets, the injustices in commerce and court, the lies and deceits, the broken relationships, the children neglected or abused. And that's not to mention the wars and bloodshed, the starvation and suffering of which we read in our headlines every day. The book of Genesis tells us that it all grieves God to his heart (Genesis 6:6). And that's the reaction that all of us often have to evil too, isn't it? We cannot help but wonder if the world will always be this way, if we always will be wearied with the unending corruption of good and decency. Certainly we saw it exhibited that day when they nailed Jesus Christ to that cross, didn't we? We human beings killed the fairest and most innocent life on the hill of Golgotha.

But the Lord God of the universe, who so hates human evil, also triumphed over that attempt to defeat his goodness. He raised his Son from the dead on the third day of the week at dawn, and he thereby showed to us that the wrong and the ruin in our world will not have the last word. No. God's is the last Word, good Christians. God's is the final victory. God's goodness, God's love, incarnated in Jesus Christ — God's good plan for his universe cannot be defeated. And you and I can live with the certain and joyful knowledge that his rule over all will come.

In fact, we can live now with the knowledge that God also can triumph over the sin and guilt that we know lurk in our own hearts. We try to ignore that guilty burden that we carry around inside of us, don't we? But sometimes, in our isolated moments, or in the dark of a sleepless night, it gnaws at our innards, and we know that something is wrong with our lives. Somewhere along the line, we made a whole series of bad choices. Somehow we're not what we were meant to be. And we wish that we had the power within ourselves to set it all right.

But the message of our text is that the resurrection means forgiveness, too. Did you catch that in the last sentence of our reading from Acts? "Every one who believes in him receives forgiveness of sins through his name" (v. 43). Everyone who trusts in God's act in Jesus Christ has a new beginning. The old is done away; behold, the new has come (2 Corinthians 5:17). And we are given a fresh start, and a new Spirit who is the Spirit of the living Christ working in us to make us into new persons, able to be good and do it.

113

That message is for everyone this morning, whether you are good or bad, believing or unbelieving before, sinner or saint, guilty or innocent in the sight of God. Jesus Christ has been raised from the dead, and God has won the victory. You need not die eternally. The evil in our world does not have the last word. All your sins and all your faults can be forgiven by God. And you can become new persons in the power of the Lord who raised his Son. It's a message for every one of us on this Easter morn. We have only to hear and take it into our hearts. And then we can truly rejoice, every one of us, on this Easter day.

Second Sunday of Easter

Acts 2:14a, 22-32

Three important religious festivals are prescribed for Israel in the Old Testament — Tabernacles in the fall, Passover in the spring, and fifty weeks later the Feast of Weeks, or what the New Testament calls Pentecost. It is during this latter religious celebration of Pentecost that the story in our text takes place.

According to the law of Deuteronomy, all Israelites journeyed to Jerusalem to celebrate their religious festivals, and so in our story, the apostles and followers of Jesus and many other devout Jews are gathered together in Jerusalem. Suddenly the Holy Spirit descends upon the disciples in tongues of fire, and they begin to speak in other tongues, so that travelers from every nation hear the disciples speaking to them in their own language, proclaiming the mighty works that God has done. It is such an astounding phenomenon that many in the crowd think that the disciples are drunk. But Peter refutes that charge and declares to the crowd that the ancient prophecy of Joel is coming true. Before the coming of the Kingdom of God, Joel had promised, God would pour out his Spirit on the faithful in Israel, enabling them to prophesy. That, Peter declares, is what is happening there in Jerusalem. The "last days" are upon them. The Kingdom of God is breaking into history. Therefore all persons should repent and call on the name of the Lord and be saved in his judgment.

Such is the account in Acts up to the beginning of our stated reading for the morning. Having explained what is happening, the Apostle Peter then proceeds to preach a sermon that connects the event with Jesus Christ, for it is with the appearance of Jesus that the new age of the kingdom has begun (cf. Luke 11:20; Mark 1:15).

Who is Jesus Christ? That is what Peter wants to explain to the crowd of Jews in his sermon. The listening Jews are familiar with the stories circulating about Jesus' works and healings and miracles, but there are lots of miracle-workers and magicians and sages in

115

first century Jerusalem. What makes Jesus so different? The answer is clear — the resurrection. This man, who was "crucified and killed by the hands of lawless men," God raised from the dead. Death could not hold him, because God is more powerful that all the forces of death.

To support his point, Peter therefore quotes verses 8-11 from Psalm 16, which tradition assigns to David. The Psalm states that God would not abandon his Holy One to death. But David died, and all the Jews present know where he is buried. The Psalm therefore is speaking not of David, but rather it is prophesying the resurrection of Jesus Christ. In Christ alone, God has fulfilled his promise that there will never be lacking a davidic heir, a Messiah, to sit upon the throne (cf. 2 Samuel 7). Christ has been raised (Acts 2:25-32). Moreover he has ascended to the position of power, to the right hand of God, and he is the one who has poured out his Spirit there on the disciples on the day of Pentecost. God has made Jesus Christ therefore both Lord and Messiah, "this Jesus whom you crucified" (vv. 33-36; the lesson really should include these verses).

It is notable in this sermon by Peter that he connects the death and resurrection of Jesus Christ with the Old Testament, not only because Peter is speaking to Jews, but because the identity of our Lord cannot fully be understood except in connection with that Book of the Old Covenant. Jesus is not some new figure suddenly dropped from the blue. Rather, his life, death, and resurrection form the final and full interpretation of all that has gone before in Israel's history. Jesus is the one who fulfills the plan and promises of God given in the past history of Israel. His death on the cross was not an accident perpetrated by sinful human beings. Rather it was foreknown, foretold in the Old Testament (cf. Isaiah 52:13—53:12), and fore-planned by God as the way to atone for the sins of the world. And the fact that he was raised by God from the dead was not a myth dreamed up by those who felt the spirit of a dead Jesus was somehow still with them. Rather it was an historical event that was foretold by "David" and witnessed to by those who met the risen Christ alive.

If we preserve that historical connection of Jesus with the Old Testament history and listen to the witness of the apostles in the

New Testament, we are prevented from distorting the figure of our Lord. He cannot be seen as a myth, as an imaginary ideal, or as nothing more than a peasant revolutionary or traveling sage or mystic visionary, as some would like to make him. No. He is the flesh and blood descendant of Abraham and David, who walked the dusty roads of Palestine in the first century A.D., who healed the sick and raised the dead and announced the arrival of the Kingdom of God, who was crucified on a Roman cross, and who on the first day of the week was raised from the dead by the power of God.

The content of the Christian faith is finally made up of a story, of a real history. And it is part of that history that Peter recounts to his listeners in Jerusalem. Our faith is not based simply on propositions — on statements such as "God is love," or "Christ died for our sins," or "The Bible is the Word of God." We believe all of those things, but the content of them is spelled out in a history. What manner of love does God have for us? We find out if we read the story! What are our sins and how and why did Christ die for them? Only the story can tell us! Why is the Bible the word of God? God speaks to us through its pages only when we read in faith! Our Christian faith rests on knowing the story, and so Peter tells some of that history in his sermon to convert his listeners. And we, when we say, "I believe," have to tell the story: "I believe in Jesus Christ, the only Son of the Father, who was born of the Virgin Mary, suffered under Pontius Pilate, was crucified, dead, and buried. He descended into hell. The third day he rose again from the dead. He ascended into heaven, and sitteth on the right hand of God the Father Almighty; from thence he shall come to judge the quick and the dead." Only on the basis of that account can we say, "I believe."

If we want to spread the Christian faith, to join those "witnesses" of whom Peter speaks in his sermon (v. 32), then we must know and tell, as did those disciples at Pentecost, "the mighty works of God" (v. 11) — the events, the history, the story of what God did through 2,000 years of history, in Israel and the early church, and what he is still doing today. He pours out the Spirit of Christ upon us, good Christians. Let us use it to proclaim his glorious deeds.

117

Third Sunday of Easter

Acts 2:14a, 36-41

Picking up where we ended our reading last week, we continue this morning with Acts' account of Peter's sermon to the assembled Jews on the day of Pentecost.

Strangely, the lectionary last Sunday was supposed to end with verse 32, and then the reading this morning begins with verse 36. But the intervening verses 33-35 are extremely important for understanding what is happening. We therefore mentioned them briefly last week and will reiterate their meaning again this week.

Because of his resurrection (v. 32; cf. Philippians 2:9), Jesus Christ has been shown to be both Lord and Christ, the Ruler of the new age of the Kingdom of God, who has been exalted in his ascension to the right hand of God, and who shares in the power of the Father. With Christ's appearance, the powers of the new age have broken into human history, his Spirit has been poured out upon his disciples gathered together, and the "last days," before the last judgment and the full coming of the kingdom, of which the prophet Joel foretold, have begun. Yet, Peter tells the assembly, you crucified that Lord (v. 36). You tried to put to death the One who is now risen Lord and Messiah over all. You face condemnation in the final judgment.

Such a message does not go over well with a modern congregation, of course. Ours is a society that, on the whole, does not believe that God judges anyone. God is a loving, forgiving, comforting God, who makes us feel better about ourselves. Self-esteem and therapeutic assurances rule our day. And salvation is equivalent to getting ourselves together.

But the scriptures are quite sure that God is moving human history toward the goal of his kingdom and that before that final coming, we will all face the question of how we stand in relation to Jesus Christ. "We must all appear before the judgment seat of

Christ," Paul writes, "so that each one may receive good or evil according to what he has done in the body" (2 Corinthians 4:10).

Peter's audience of devout Jews in our scripture lesson know that God's judgment is coming, and so their reaction to Peter's account of the resurrection and lordship of Christ, and their realization that they have been among those who crucified him, cuts them "to the heart" (v. 37). "Brethren, what shall we do?" they cry out to Peter and the apostles.

Peter's answer is immediate. "Repent, and be baptized every one of you in the name of Jesus Christ for the forgiveness of your sins; and you shall receive the gift of the Holy Spirit" (v. 38). Repentance for sin in trust in Christ, baptism, receipt of the enabling Spirit of good — those define the crowd's path to salvation in the last judgment (cf. v. 40).

That action that Peter prescribes is not to be taken as the absolute order that we are to follow. After all, most of you here this morning have already been baptized. And with your baptism we believe you have received the Holy Spirit. The church has always considered that baptism and the receipt of the Spirit are given simultaneously. But obviously all of us here this morning have need of repentance — repentance for things we have done or left undone during this past week, repentance for our past and our proclivities to go our own way instead of God's, repentance for the fact that we have not loved our God with all our heart and soul and mind and strength, or our neighbor as ourselves. We all stand in need of repentance.

The important note in our text is that little phrase "in the name of Jesus Christ" (v. 38). Always the forgiveness of our sins and our restoration to relation with our God is dependent on Jesus Christ. He is the only one by whom we can be justified and counted righteous in the eyes of our God. He is the only one who can redeem us from our sin and from eternal death. He is the only one who can present us blameless before the bar of God in the final judgment. Trust in the forgiving and saving work of Jesus Christ — that is the foundation of Christian discipleship. That is the action by which we can be saved. And trust means that we count no longer upon our own abilities to justify and save ourselves, but that we count

120

solely upon our Lord. We throw ourselves totally upon his mercy — "Lord, be merciful to me a sinner" (Luke 18:13). And he who is forgiving Love beyond all of our imagining, declares us righteous inheritors of eternal life.

Note too in our text that when Peter tells the assembled crowd what they must do, he also proclaims to them that the promise of salvation is not only to them, assembled there is Jerusalem that day, but "the promise is to you and to your children and to all that are far off" (v. 39). The promise of salvation is to every generation of every nation that has lived or that shall live since Peter preached in Jerusalem. The promise is to us gathered here this morning. There are no barriers to the love of God in Jesus Chrst, no barriers of race or status, of gender or condition, of class or previous unworthiness. God loves his world, every single, sinful, hurting, hungering one of us. And in his Son our Lord, God offers us reconciliation and return to his beloved company and to the joy of our Father's house.

Another note in our text: "The promise is to you and to your children" (v. 39). Our little children, our sons and daughters whom we love so very much, are loved also by the Lord of us all and called to trust in him. And we can aid that trust by telling them the story of what God in Christ has done. Are you teaching your children the story that is found in the Bible? Are you passing on to them the language of our faith? Are you accompanying them to church school and worship, and teaching them how to pray? And very important, are you praying every day also for them? For God wants to welcome them, along with you, into his kingdom of eternal life.

Finally, note that our text says that the promise is to "every one whom the Lord calls to him" (v. 39). By that sentence, Peter is saying that even our trust in Christ is not our own doing. Rather, it too is a gift of God's Holy Spirit. God does it all for us, good Christians. He calls us, forgives us, justifies us, receives us, all that we may have life and have it eternally. Thanks be to God for his inestimable gift through Jesus Christ our Lord!

Fourth Sunday of Easter

Acts 2:42-47

These stories in Acts about the beginning of the church in Jerusalem are intended by Luke, the author of Acts, to tell of the powerful work of the Holy Spirit. So it is that after Peter's sermon concerning the resurrection of Christ, which we looked at last Sunday, we read in Acts 2:41 that "there were added that day about three thousand souls" to the fellowship of the church.

These conversions were no momentary outbursts of enthusiasm, however, that had no effect on the lives of those who believed and were baptized. Rather, in our text for the morning, Acts immediately goes on to tell us about the changes that were wrought in the lives of the new Christians. Belief brought about transformation, as true faith always does.

We learn first, therefore, that all of these new Jerusalem Christians were bound together in a community, in a church, if you will — not like our churches with buildings and ministers, educational programs and weekly worship services, but a church nevertheless. The work of the Spirit produced a new fellowship that probably met in various-sized groups in persons' houses, since most of the New Testament churches were house churches (cf. Romans 16:3-5). These early Christians had placed their trust in a risen Lord who had taught them to forgive and minister to and love one another. And the Holy Spirit of Christ produced that love and caring among them. They became persons who bore one another's burdens (cf. Galatians 6:2), who took an interest in each other's welfare, and who gave of their time and labor for one another. They became a community truly living by the Spirit of Christ.

The amazing result, therefore, as verses 44 and 45 tell us, is that they "had all things in common. They sold their possessions and goods and distributed them to all, as any had need." Now those verses disturb us modern-day Christians a great deal, don't they, because they seem to suggest a communist or socialist way of life. Or if we take them personally, they run up against our strong objections to their implications for us materially wealthy and comfortable church members. We have no intention of selling all we have and of distributing the profits among our fellow Christians. We are very much like that rich young man in Jesus' story in Mark, whom our Lord commanded to "go, sell what you have, and give to the poor ... and come, follow me" (Mark 10:17-22). We, too, go away sorrowful, because we have "great possessions."

But I think we have to get at the basic thrust of this description of the early Jerusalem church in Acts in verses 44 and 45 of our text. It is not laying upon the necessity of a communal society in America. Rather, what it is saying is that those early Christians were conscious of and ministered to the material needs of one another. They loved one another, and so they did not let any one of their fellowship want for the necessities of life. They gave to those "who had need." And that is the responsibility laid upon us also — to give generously to those in need, wherever they may be in the far-flung reaches of the church. There should be no one hungry or unable to provide for their children or lacking proper shelter and clothing in the Christian Church. We must not ignore others' basic needs. In whatever way we meet those necessities, by whatever mission giving or financial method or plan of employment, one of the marks of true Christian fellowship is concern, not for our own comfort, but for the welfare of our fellow believers.

Our passage lays out other characteristics of that early Jerusalem church that was formed by the Spirit of Christ. "They devoted themselves," says verse 42, "to the apostles' teaching." And that is an integral part of Christian life in the church — teaching, learning, education. But their education was not simply a discussion of the problems of their society, as so much of our education is. Nor was it designed to be simply inspirational or therapeutic, as again ours often is. No, it was study of the apostles' teaching. In other words, it was a study of what Peter and Paul, James and Philip, and the other apostles had proclaimed about Jesus Christ. In addition, it was a study of Jesus' words and deeds as those related to the Old Testament, which was the Bible of the early church. They studied what we now have written in our Bibles: that is the apostolic teaching. They learned what God had done in the history of Israel and of Jesus Christ, and they discussed and meditated and memorized those mighty, saving acts.

That is indeed a model for our church life, isn't it, because the foundation of our faith consists in the accounts of the words and deeds of God found now in our Old and New Testaments. Those words alone, illumined by the Holy Spirit, tell us who God truly is and what he desires and what he is doing. Those words alone can anchor our faith firmly in the way, the truth, and the life, and give us the knowledge that must accompany our religious zeal. Without knowledge, Christian faith dies, and most of us unfortunately are lacking in that basic knowledge. If we want to be the church, we must devote ourselves to the apostles' teaching, now found in our scriptures.

That early Jerusalem church also worshiped together. They participated in the "breaking of bread," which is probably a reference to the Lord's Supper (v. 42), for Luke earlier tells us that the disciples first knew the risen Christ in "the breaking of bread" (Luke 24:35). And we know him there too, do we not? In our celebration of the Lord's Supper together, the risen Christ comes to us once again in the Spirit, and pours out his vitality and power upon us, and binds us together with himself and the Father, with one another, and with all of the faithful through the ages. Finally our faith finds it empowering motivation in our communion with our Lord and one another. And without that relation to our Lord, we cannot be Christians.

Those forbears of our faith in Jerusalem also prayed together (v. 42), lifting up their praises and thanksgivings (v. 46), their confessions and penitence, their petitions for themselves and other to God through Christ. Their prayer was the response to all that God did for them, and our prayers are our response also. God in Christ in the Spirit has done all things for us. In prayer we give back our thanks and the concerns of our daily lives, laying all out before him in our surrender to his love.

It is no wonder that Acts can tell us that group of early Christians in Jerusalem could perform wonders in their community

(v. 43). After all, they lived in the power of God, and it is no wonder that they found favor among the people, or that numbers of converts were added to their fellowship day by day (v. 47). They lived and moved and had their being in the Spirit of Christ that had been poured out on them. They truly were a church, and that is the community we too can be if we let the Lord Christ has his way with us.

Fifth Sunday of Easter

Acts 7:55-60

I got in a religious dispute one time with a relative over particular truths in the Christian gospel, and at one point in the argument, as she became more and more defensive, she blurted out, "Don't quote scripture to me!"

We don't like it very much when the very faith that we profess is used against us to show us that we are wrong. After all, faith is a good thing, and our piety is sincere, and we don't want anyone telling us, by means of the faith, that we're on the wrong track in what we believe and how we act. Indeed, nothing is quite so enraging as to have our beliefs turned against us.

That's exactly why Stephen, a second generation Christian in Jerusalem, is stoned to death, however. He uses the beliefs of his fellow Jews to convict them. When his compatriots can't best him in religious arguments (Acts 6:10) or put down the wonders and signs that he does among the people (6:8), they get a bunch of thugs to accuse Stephen falsely of speaking blasphemy against Moses and the law, and against God and the temple (6:11-14). As a result, Stephen is hauled before the council of the Sanhedrin that was made up in Jerusalem of priests, rulers, elders, and scribes, and he is queried as to whether or not the charges are true (7:1).

In answer, Stephen's face is like the face of an angel — Luke's indication that Stephen is speaking in the power of the Holy Spirit (6:15) — and the address that Stephen gives is the longest speech to be found in Acts — an indication of its importance. What Stephen does is to recount the Old Testament's traditions concerning the patriarchs, Joseph, Moses, the law, and Solomon's construction of the temple. And some of the words in the account quote portions of the Old Testament rather closely. But as he recites the tradition of God's acts of salvation, Stephen uses that very tradition to accuse his fellow Jews of faithlessness.

Stephen's opponents are very concerned about Moses and the law, but their forbears refused to obey Moses and broke the law by worshiping the golden calf (7:35-43, 53). They are deeply attached to their temple, but the temple cannot house the God who has heaven for his throne and earth for his footstool (7:47-50). And they continued to be apostate by persecuting the prophets who foretold the coming of the Righteous One, Jesus Christ, God's intended Messiah. More than that, the present listeners have murdered that promised Son of God (7:51-53).

In making those charges, Stephen employs the very heart of the Jewish faith — the law by which every Jew is supposed to live; the cult through which the Jews have communion with their God, and the prophets who pronounce God's Word to the people. You Jews, Stephen preaches, have been faithless toward all three. Your religion is phony, you stand condemned in the sight of your God, and your execution of God's Son has revealed the final extent of your sin.

If someone made the same accusation against us, we too would be enraged. Imagine someone saying to us, "You're practice of your faith is as phony as a three dollar bill." But it is when Stephen makes his final statement that the lynch mob hauls him out of the city to be stoned. I saw the glory of God, he says, and the Son of Man, Jesus, standing at his right hand of power. In short, Stephen states that Jesus Christ has been raised and has been exalted by God to rule over all (7:56). Jesus Christ now reigns supreme over law and cult and prophets. Jesus Christ is now Lord. That is the last blasphemous straw, the message to which the mob shuts its ears and rushes to do away with the messenger.

The witnesses who have made the accusation against Stephen join in his stoning, shedding their cloaks at the feet of a Pharisee named Saul — the first mention of that figure who is to dominate Acts' story from here on.

As the stones strike Stephen, knocking him to the ground, he does not cry out against his executioners, but instead prays to Jesus, whom he has testified to be the Lord. The words that he prays imitate his Lord's words on the cross. Quoting Psalm 31, Jesus had prayed, "Father, into thy hands I commit my spirit" (Luke 23:46).

Stephen too delivers his life into the hands of his Lord, in the sure knowledge of his resurrection (Acts 7:59). Jesus had prayed as he was nailed to the wood, "Father, forgive them for they know not what they do" (Luke 23:34). Stephen, too, asks Jesus' forgiveness of the mob that is killing him. "Lord, do not hold this sin against them" (Acts 7:60). In life and in death, the pattern for Stephen's life is Jesus Christ. He dies, faithful to his Lord.

Luke uses this story of the martyrdom of Stephen to show, in the Roman empire, that the Christian faith is an extension of Judaism and therefore not subversive to Roman rule. It is from the law and the prophets and writings of old that Jesus Christ may be understood (cf. Luke 24:44-45). The history of salvation that Stephen recounts in his long testimony finds its final fulfillment in the life, death, and resurrection of our Lord. That is a good indication to us that we cannot truly know Jesus Christ except we know also the history of the Old Testament that has preceded him. He is the final fulfillment and interpretation of that sacred history.

But the question that is directed pointedly to us on this fifth Sunday of the Easter season is: Have we been faithful to the religion that we profess as Christians? We confess that Jesus Christ is our Lord. Do we then act as if he is our Lord? Do we take our directions for life from his commandments to us? Do we try to follow his will, or is our own self-will the guide and director of our daily lives? We worship and praise him in our cult, that is, in our church services. But does our living point to his glory or to our own reputation and status? And is gratitude to God the tenor of our daily round or is it full of complaint and dissatisfaction and yearning after ever more goods and things? We believe that our Lord holds our future in his hands, as he proclaims in his prophetic words. But do we trust that future and lay aside our anxieties and fear of death in the faith that nothing can separate us from the love of God in Christ Jesus our Lord?

This account of the disciple Stephen is a call to examine our lives, and an opportunity in the power of the Spirit to cleanse our faith of falsity and phoniness.

Sixth Sunday of Easter

Acts 17:22-31

There is a strange belief abroad in our land at the present time, the belief that we cannot know God. Such a belief rises partly from a feeling of awe before the divine — the feeling that God is so unfathomable, so other, so beyond our feeble understanding that we cannot possibly experience who he truly is in all of his fullness and perfection. And perhaps that is the reason that the Athenians have erected that idol "to an unknown God" that Paul encounters when he visits their city. They know that there is a god beyond them, but they cannot define him or name him.

On the other hand, many persons use the fact that they cannot know God in his Being as an excuse for manufacturing their own gods and goddesses. And that was certainly true also of a lot of Athenians in Paul's time. They had a whole pantheon of deities, all presupposed from the ways and forces of the natural world about them. They built idols to those deities and filled the streets of Athens with them. Paul "saw that the city was full of idols," reads Acts 17:16. And Paul's "spirit was provoked within him."

Thus, when Paul argued in the synagogue and in the market-place, proclaiming Jesus Christ risen from the dead, that piqued the curiosity of the intelligentsia in Athens, the epicurean and stoic philosophers. This was something new, and they loved new fads (17:21). They gathered frequently in the Areopagus, that section of the city where philosophical debates were carried on, and there they enjoyed hearing or telling about the latest novelty, including the latest deity. Maybe this new God that Paul was preaching about was another deity that they could add to their pantheon! They really didn't believe much in their manufactured gods. But they did want to be up on the latest religious developments. No one likes to be out of touch with what is going on.

The story presents us with a picture that could almost be a portrayal of our society, for if anything characterizes modern American society, it is the search for some sort of new religion. "I'm a searcher," someone will say, and that usually means they want to know about any new religion or deity that has been invented.

Our land is full of such supposed searchers. A lot of them, like the Athenians, have constructed their beliefs on the basis of the natural world, and so they have identified the mysterious and vital forces in nature with God. And we find the worship of a Mother Goddess, or of a great Primal Matrix, or of some ancient goddess of the Near East. Others have turned to transcendental meditation, or to some Eastern guru, or to the powers in a pyramid. Some follow astrology and see their lives dependent on the planets. Some follow a self-proclaimed savior, like Sun Myung Moon or the leader of Heaven's Gate. And not a few search for the goddess, the divine, the eternal spirit within themselves, making their inner being the locus of the divine. All peoples finally hunger for some sort of an Other, and every culture has its own form of religion. But our modern society at the present time presents a picture that is "full of idols."

In their curiosity about the new God that Paul seems to be proclaiming, the philosophers of Athens summon him to the Areopagus to tell them about it, and it is to their credit that they listen carefully to his words.

Paul wrote about himself in 1 Corinthians that his preaching was always "in weakness and in fear and trembling," "not in plausible words of wisdom" (1 Corinthians 1:3-4). Nevertheless, the speech that Acts portrays Paul as delivering to the learned Athenian crowd is a model of classical rhetoric. He shapes his approach very carefully in order to win over converts.

Paul begins his oration by flattering his audience — he perceives that they are very religious — and then he starts his argument with a fact that all of the philosophers know: They did not create themselves. So Paul begins his speech where his audience is. They and he agree. Logically, it follows then that if God created humans, God is more than human and cannot be served by human means. He cannot be represented in an idol and he does not live in shrines made by human hands. Nor does he need anything that is limited to the human sphere. After all, he even made the nations and gave them their allotted territories. So he should not be reduced to human proportions. Yet, he sustains all mortals alive and is not far from anyone, giving to them life and breath and everything. All human beings live and move and have their being in him, Paul says, quoting their own poetry to the learned listeners.

So it is ignorance to worship God in an idol, Paul continues. More than that, God is no longer unknown. Rather, he has revealed himself. He does not have to be imagined by the thoughts of mortals. He has made himself known. And because of that, he now calls all people to repent of their idolatry. For a while in human history, God overlooked human ignorance. But now that he has given the revelation of himself in Jesus Christ, everyone must put away their imagined gods.

How do we know that Jesus Christ is the revelation of God? Because Christ has been raised from the dead, Paul proclaims. And the risen Christ is coming in the future to judge the world rightly and in truth. Then all will be held accountable for their worship and their faith. Thus runs the content of Paul's speech.

At the heart of Paul's preaching is the testimony to the resurrection of our Lord. Indeed, that forms the central thrust of Paul's Christian message throughout his letters. Everything hangs on that resurrection testimony to the lordship of Jesus. "If Christ has not been raised, your faith is futile and you are still in your sins" (1 Corinthians 15:17). Apart from the resurrection, there is no Christian faith.

The implication, of course, is that since we Christians are "Easter people," who have so recently celebrated the resurrection of our Lord, the time is now to put away all of our false gods and goddesses — to repent and to turn our hearts and lives to Jesus Christ alone. No more worship of the forces of nature. No more following the stars or various gurus. No more giving of our attention to the latest religious fad. Indeed, no more giving our devotion to the material things of this world, or to our own self-fulfillment, or to our own ways and thoughts. No. God has made himself known in Jesus Christ. It is in him that we live and move and have our being. He alone is the revelation of the Father. And in him alone we can have life, abundant now and blessed to all eternity.

Ascension of Our Lord

Acts 1:1-11

The book of the Acts of the Apostles is the second volume of Luke's great account of God's act of salvation in Jesus Christ. The first volume — the Gospel according to Luke — dealt with the life, death, and resurrection of our Lord. Now the second volume concerns the results of that — the formation and growth of the first-century church under the power of the Holy Spirit. Acts picks up where the Gospel left off — with the ascension of the Lord (Luke 24:51; Acts 1:9).

Before rushing in to the account of the ascension, however, Luke wants to nail down some facts. First is the fact of the resurrection. That is necessary for everything that follows. Apart from the resurrection of Christ there is no basis for faith, for the gift of the Spirit, or for the formation of the church.

In verse 3 of our text, therefore, Acts affirms that Jesus appeared alive to the apostles after his crucifixion, showing himself for forty days and teaching them further about the Kingdom of God. That affirmation is similar to the one that Paul gives in 1 Corinthians 15:5-8. Jesus Christ really has been raised from the dead! The testimony of the apostles who saw him alive after his burial is true! As in the Fourth Gospel, everything hangs on that apostolic witness (John 20:29). And their testimony is confirmed by many witnesses.

Having said that, Acts also repeats the command that Jesus gives to his disciples at the end of the Gospel (Luke 24:49) — that the apostles are to remain in Jerusalem until they receive the gift of the Holy Spirit (Acts 1:4). Only then will they be empowered to carry out their mission. The apostles and disciples are to be Christ's witnesses in all of Palestine and throughout the earth, but they cannot accomplish that task on their own power or by their own resources. They must wait for God's empowering Spirit and for the wisdom and guidance that he will give them. John's baptism furnished them with repentance and the forgiveness of their sins (Acts 1:5; Luke 3:3), but the work of the church requires much more than that. It requires empowerment.

Second, our text emphasizes the fact that there is a goal out there ahead of the church, toward which we journey. The apostles have come to realize that Jesus is the Christ, the Son of God and the long-awaited davidic Messiah of Israel. That means Christ has begun the reign of God on earth; the kingdom has begun to break into human time and space (cf. Luke 11:20). But from of old, the promise of the kingdom has always included the restoration and salvation of Israel, God's covenant people (cf. Luke 1:54, 68-75; 2:29-32; 24:21). While the risen Christ is teaching his apostles during his forty days with them, they therefore ask their Lord about that goal, about the time when the Kingdom of God will come in its fullness and all Israel will be saved (Acts 1:6; cf. Romans 11:26). It is the same question that we still ask: When will the Second Coming take place; when will Christ return to set up his kingdom on earth?

Acts' version of Christ's answer to the question is the same as we find recorded in the Synoptic Gospels. "It is not for you to know" (Acts 1:7). Only the Father knows. As it is written in the Gospel according to Mark, "Of that day or that hour, no one knows, not even the angels in heaven, nor the Son, but only the Father" (Mark 13:32). It is certain that the Kingdom of God is coming on earth "even as it is in heaven." But when the kingdom will be established by the Father is known only to that Father. The apostles' task, and ours, is therefore not to try to calculate the time of the end, but to be about our Father's business of being his witnesses throughout all the world.

Having said that, our text continues, the Lord is lifted up and taken out of the apostles' sight (Acts 1:9). And that is our text's third emphasis in this passage — the fact that the Lord Jesus Christ has ascended to be with the Father. The implication is, as we read before in Acts 7:55, that Christ now reigns at the right hand of power as Lord over all the earth.

136

Certainly this account of the ascension of our Lord, as in Luke 24:51, is incomprehensible to us, especially in our scientific age when we know that "heaven" is no longer "up." We will always speak of it that way, of course, because our thought deals in spatial categories. But the ascension affirms that the realm of God is totally other than our human realm — that it is another world which our senses cannot penetrate and which is known to us only by faith. We have sometimes sensed that "other world" in the exaltation of worship, as if we were standing with one foot in heaven. But that sense too is given us only by faith.

The principal fact of which the ascension assures us, however, is that our Lord is no longer limited by a physical body or by geographical location or local time, but now reigns as Lord over all of creation to all eternity.

It is interesting in our text that the disciples are as mystified by Christ's disappearance into heaven as are we (Acts 1:10). They stand gazing upwards, wondering. But two angels, clothed in white (cf. Luke 24:4), ask them why they are just standing there gazing up into the sky (v. 11). Christ is ascended. This is no time to be standing around. He will come again. But in the meantime, the apostles have work to do. They are to remain in Jerusalem and wait for their empowerment by the Spirit. And then they are to go out into all the world and witness to what God has done in the life, death, and resurrection of Jesus Christ.

We might say that this text in Acts furnishes us with the bedrock of our life in the church. It affirms that Jesus Christ is risen from the dead and has ascended into heaven as the Lord over all. It warns us against idle speculation about those facts and instead, spells out their implication for us in the church. Our church membership is not just a matter of having our sins forgiven for another week and then returning home and going about our normal business. No. We have work to do. Christ has appointed us as the witnesses to what God has done for all people throughout the world. But we cannot carry out that witness on our own. No matter how big or small our congregation. No matter how rich or resourceful we are. No matter what the marvelous programs of our church, or

137

how enthusiastic its life, we do not have the ability or strength within ourselves to accomplish on our own the task that God has given us. We are dependent on God's Spirit to be what he has chosen us to be. And that leads us to the question that we should always ask: Have we been given the Holy Spirit?

Seventh Sunday of Easter

Acts 1:6-14

Our reading for this Sunday includes verses 6 to 11, which were part of our stated text for last Sunday. The preacher, therefore, has to remind the congregation of what has happened. The apostles have asked Jesus when he will restore the kingdom to Israel, that is, when will the Kingdom of God come. Jesus has replied that the time of that coming is not for them — or even him — to know, thus ending all of the church's speculation about the time of the end. The Lord has promised that the fledgling group will receive the gift of the Holy Spirit, which will empower them to become his witnesses throughout the world. And then Christ has been "lifted up" in his ascension, to rule at the right hand of God over all. Two angels therefore bid the apostles to stop gazing up into heaven. It is time to get to work.

It is interesting in our text for the morning that the ascension has taken place on the Mount of Olives, that mountain across the Kidron Valley to the east of Jerusalem that towers up over the height of Mount Zion. Olivet has great significance in both Old and New Testaments. It is the watchtower from which all attacks against Jerusalem were visible. But it is probably the mountain from which Second Isaiah told the people that they would see God returning to them (Isaiah 40:9-11), and Revelation probably means that it is from Olivet that the faithful will see the descent of the heavenly Jerusalem (Revelation 21:10). Jesus pronounced judgment over Jerusalem from the mount (Mark 13:3). And it is the site of the Garden of Gethsemane (Mark 13:3 and parallels). Most significant as background of this Acts text, however, is the fact that Ezekiel pictured God's glory as departing from the Mount of Olives and then, later in the eschatological time, returning to it, to enter from there into Jerusalem (Ezekiel 11:23; 43:2). The implication is that

Jesus' ascension not only takes place from the Mount of Olives, but it is there that he will return when he comes again.

Because the angels tell the apostles not to stand gazing into heaven, the apostles descend from Olivet and return to Jerusalem, a hike which Luke says is "a sabbath day's journey away" (v. 12). That would have no significance if it were not for the fact that Jews do not journey on the sabbath! That's against the Jewish law! And so by this little phrase Luke is telling us that we have a new people here, folk who have known the resurrected Christ and whose lives have been changed, to be given a task of going into all the world and preaching the good news about Jesus Christ. The company is named — the eleven apostles who remain after Judas Iscariot's betrayal (Luke 23:47-48; Luke says nothing about Iscariot's death, but cf. Matthew 27:3-5 and Acts 1:16-19). In the passage that follows in verses 15-26, Iscariot will be replaced by Matthias in the company of the twelve.

This is the tiny band of those who will begin the spread of the gospel throughout the earth. Noteworthy is the fact that they are joined by some women. Luke repeatedly includes women in his stories of Jesus, and these in our text are probably the women who were earlier mentioned in Luke's Gospel — the women whom Jesus healed and who supported his ministry financially (Luke 8:2-3); the women who did not desert their Lord at his crucifixion and burial (Luke 23:49, 55-56); and who were the first witnesses of the resurrection to the disbelieving apostles (Luke 24:1-11). Included also are Mary, the mother of Jesus, and his brothers, of whom we have heard earlier in Luke 1-2 and 8:19-21. So the little band of apostles is enlarged by others who have known Jesus and who love him.

When we in the church in our day are given a task to do, or appointed to a committee, or singled out for leadership, our tendency is to jump right to it, to get to work. A pastor who has just been called by a church is often heard to say, "I hit the ground running." But this group of apostles and disciples in our Acts text don't jump immediately into their task and start running. They're down on their knees praying! They have returned to the upper room in Jerusalem where the apostles have been lodging, and there they all unite together in prayer (vv. 12-14).

For what do they pray? Acts does not tell us, but it is clear from the preceding verses. Their risen Lord has commanded them to return to Jerusalem and to wait for the Holy Spirit to come upon them. So they pray for that Spirit's coming. Only then will they be able to be his witnesses in Jerusalem and throughout Palestine and the known world. They are obeying their Lord's command. From the very first, they are faithful to the word of the risen and ascended Christ. From this time on, their lives have changed, to let Christ rule over them. And so they are faithful to his lordship.

They also are a band pressing forward toward the coming of the kingdom — toward that time when Christ will return to set up his rule over all the earth (cf. Acts 1:6). They therefore undoubtedly pray for the coming of that kingdom. "Our Father ... thy kingdom come on earth, even as it is in heaven." The apostles and disciples are the messengers of that kingdom, the ones who are to announce to the world, "Behold! the Lord God comes with might, and his arm rules for him" (Isaiah 40:10). Prepare, therefore, for his coming! "The kingdom of God is at hand; repent, and believe the gospel" (Mark 1:15).

The message that we modern disciples are given to announce to the world is not a great deal different than that. Our Lord Christ is risen and ascended and reigns over all. And he will come again "to judge the quick and the dead." But by faith in Christ's work of reconciliation through his death and resurrection, we can know the forgiveness of all our sins and be counted righteous in the sight of our God and enter into eternal life in his kingdom of love.

To be faithful messengers of that good news, however, we must learn to wait, as the apostles and disciples waited. Not jumping immediately into the task of each day, not running around in the busyness of the church, but first praying — praying for God's empowering Spirit that can enable us to be obedient and to do his will and to accomplish the purposes for which he has called us. We do not own the Holy Spirit. For each task given us as disciples, we must ask anew for God's guidance and empowerment. And if we ask, in faith and sincerity, the Spirit will be given to us (cf. Luke 11:9-13). So first pray. Then work. God will do the rest.

Pentecost

Acts 2:1-21

On the previous Sundays of this Eastertide, we have heard the risen Christ tell his followers to remain in Jerusalem until he sends the Holy Spirit upon them. That will enable them to be his witnesses in Jerusalem and Judea and Samaria, and to the ends of the earth. Having promised that, he ascended into heaven, to rule over all at the right hand of the Father. That promise was spoken during the forty days that the Lord was with the apostles and disciples after his resurrection.

Now, in our text for the morning, the Lord keeps his promise. It is the day of Pentecost, that is, the day of the Jewish festival celebrating the wheat harvest, which falls fifty days after Passover and, in our calendar, after Easter. So the apostles and disciples have been waiting ten days for the fulfillment of Christ's promise. During that time, they have been at prayer, praying for the fulfillment of the promise that their Lord has given them.

Jesus Christ always keeps his promises. When Christ's followers are all gathered together in one place, probably in prayer, there are the sound of a mighty wind rushing upon them and tongues of fire resting on each of their heads. And they begin to speak in the various languages that were current throughout the Mediterranean world, telling about the mighty acts that God has wrought in the life of Israel and of Jesus Christ. As a result, the devout Jews from all over the Near Eastern world, who have come to Jerusalem for the festival, hear the disciples speaking to them in their own languages. The miracle is one of speaking and of hearing.

Who can say exactly what happened at Pentecost? We are as amazed by the account as were those Jews who experienced it, and like them, we try to give a naturalistic explanation for the happening. "They're drunk," some of the Jews said, "babbling in their stupor." We like to scale down the miracles recorded in the scriptures to our level of understanding.

Whatever we think about this text, however, certainly it is meant to convey three facts. First of all, its author Luke intends it to be a reversal of the biblical account of the Tower of Babel, in Genesis 11:1-9. In that Old Testament story, God brought his judgment upon the sins of all of us — for it is our story — by confusing our language and scattering us abroad upon the face of the earth. That is, our sin brought upon us the destruction of human community. And we have only to read the morning headlines to see how true that is. We can't get along with one another any more. Nations can't understand one another's language or live in peace with one another.

But now, here in the story of Pentecost, that confusion of language and the strife between nations is overcome by the gift of the Holy Spirit. And Acts is telling us that it is the Spirit, prompting the proclamation of the gospel, that can overcome the brokenness of human community and our sinful inability to understand one another and live at peace. As Paul earlier put it, "There is neither Jew nor Greek, there is neither slave nor free, there is neither male nor female, so you are all one in Christ Jesus" (Galatians 3:28). By the work of the Holy Spirit of Christ our warring madness can be overcome.

Second, the author of our text is certainly pointing to the fulfillment of Christ's promise to his followers. Christ has not left us desolate; he has come to us, as the Fourth Gospel would put it (John 14:18). He promised that if we would wait for him, he would send his Holy Spirit to be with us — his abiding presence. And now to his fledgling church, he keeps that promise. The rushing wind and the tongues of fire are symbolic of the Spirit's presence.

But where do we receive the Holy Spirit? Has the gift been given to us, too? Yes, indeed! When each of you was baptized, the water poured upon you was the outward symbol of that gift, and all of you now are recipients of the Spirit of your Lord Christ. The power of God in Christ has been given to every one of us and to this church's congregation.

That has tremendous implications. It means that we now are enabled to be Christ's witnesses to the ends of the earth, obeying our Lord's command to go into all the world and to make disciples of all nations. We have been empowered, as were the first apostles and disciples, and as every Christian since has been empowered to tell of the mighty acts of God — not only through our missionaries, but individually, to our neighbors and families, our social circle and city, our state, and our nation. And we become those witnesses, acting in the power of the Holy Spirit, not only by what we say, but also by what we do everyday — in home and business, school, and social circles. "You are my witnesses," our Lord says to us, and we, in his Spirit, now have the power and the ability to fulfill that role. In the Spirit granted to us, we can live Christian lives and thereby witness to the world what God is able to do for all people.

Third, as our text proceeds, it is also clear that Luke intends this account of Pentecost to be the fulfillment of the prophecy of the Old Testament. The prophet Joel, back in the fifth century B.C., had proclaimed to Israel that the Day of the Lord was coming (cf. Joel 1:15; 2:1-2) — that day when God would bring his last judgment upon all humankind, that day when the Lord would separate the sheep from the goats and do away with his enemies and take into his kingdom those who had been faithful to him (cf. Matthew 25:31-46). But before that fearful day came, Joel had promised, God would pour out his Spirit on young and old, and those of high and low estate, and all in the covenant people. But, the prophet announced, all who turned to God in faith and worship would be saved in the final judgment (cf. Joel 2:28-32).

That prophecy, proclaims Peter in our text, has now come to pass. God has put his Spirit upon the followers of Jesus Christ. But that means, you see, that the Day of the Lord still lies ahead of us in our history. We have been made recipients of the Holy Spirit. That is a foresign of the final end of our history, of the time when God will, indeed, come in judgment to separate the evil from the good, and give everlasting life to his own. How can we stand before that judgment? In Christ. Through our faith in the love of God in Jesus Christ, who has forgiven us and reconciled us to the Father, and, despite all of our sins and weakness, promised us eternal life in his good kingdom.

So this day of Pentecost brings us a wondrous fact, good Christians — the fact that we have been given the Holy Spirit to enable us to be Christ's witnesses — to take a gospel to all the world that can heal the nations, and that can offer to all persons everywhere their salvation in the final judgment.

Trinity Sunday

Genesis 1:1 — 2:4a

This priestly account of God's creation of the world has been called the most theological chapter in the whole Bible. Written down in the sixth century B.C., its every word is carefully thought through. But it is not intended to be a scientific account of how God made the cosmos. The endless creationist attempts to make it into science and to foist it on our schools are invalid.

Rather, this passage is intended as a confession of faith. Some of its language is borrowed from other ancient Near Eastern religions. But the borrowed words and phrases of the time are only utilized to set forth a soaring faith that arises out of Israel's historical experience with her God. Because God has had the power to roll back the waters of the Reed Sea and to set his people free from slavery; because he has had the might to kill and to make alive, to overcome the mightiest empires, and to make for himself a chosen people, Israel has confessed that the Lord has sovereignty over all things and persons as their Creator and Sustainer. We must not ignore the faith exhibited in this passage in favor of some sort of ignorant "science."

God's creative act in this text consists in bringing order into the darkness, evil, and death of chaos, symbolized here in the form of the watery deep. In the beginning, says our text, there was only *tohu wabbohu*, formlessness and void — the all-engulfing powers of nothingness. And God's act of creation consisted in putting bounds on chaos and holding it in check, so that the life and light, order and goodness of creation become possible for humans and all things (cf. Psalm 104:5-9; Job 38:8-11; Isaiah 45:18-19). Thus, God creates light to hold back the darkness, and separates the chaotic waters by dividing them with the solid arc of the firmament. He puts bounds on the chaos to let the dry land appear, and captures the chaos below the solid earth. Then there is room for God

147

to bring forth by his word plants and trees, sun and moon and stars, animals of every kind, and finally human beings.

In short, the confession of faith here is that God is not only the Creator of all, but that he also sustains the life and order of everything. The chaos can return (cf. Genesis 7:11; Job 3:8; Jeremiah 4:23-26), and it is only because God holds it in check by his faithfulness that it does not engulf the creation. We are dependent on the Lord for the very structure and sustenance of our universe.

There therefore is no deism here. God does not just wind up the world like a watchmaker and then let it run by itself according to what we call natural laws. No. It is by the Word of God that plants and trees, animals and human beings can bring forth fruit according to their kind and propagate the earth. Nature's processes continue because God speaks their continuance, and then adds his special blessing to allow their ongoing existence (vv. 22, 28; cf. Genesis 8:22).

Two kinds of light are created according to our text. There is the light of verse 3, that is given by the Word of God. And then there is the light shed by the sun and moon and stars (vv. 16-18). Throughout the Bible, the light furnished by the Word of God is given only to the faithful (cf. Exodus 10:21-23; Job 29:2-3; Psalm 36:9; Isaiah 2:5; Matthew 5:14; Romans 13:12; etc.), and finally finds its incarnation in Jesus Christ, who is the light and life of human beings (John 1:4, 9). The other kind of light, furnished by the heavenly bodies is given to all persons (cf. Matthew 5:45). And in a little phrase, the text makes fun of those who follow astrology and worship the stars. "He made the stars also," says verse 16 — just a little after-thought on God's part, who rules over all the heavenly bodies.

The high point of creation, according to our text, is the creation of human beings, both male and female. And they are distinguished from all other creatures by the fact that they are made in the image of God (vv. 26-27). In the Old Testament, only the priestly primeval history asserts that fact (cf. Genesis 5:1; 9:6). And in the Old Testament as contrasted with the New, the image does not signify moral perfection. In the New Testament, only Christ bears the uncorrupted image (cf. Colossians 1:15; 2 Corinthians 3:18), but

148

in the Old Testament, all human beings bear it, even after the fall (cf. Genesis 9:6).

Once again we have a confession of faith. Our text is saying that we all stand inextricably related to God and are responsible to him. We cannot fully be understood, except there is included that relationship to our Creator and Lord. Therefore, in everything that we do and say and think, we are doing and saying and thinking it in relationship to the Lord who made us. There is no way we can stand outside of the relationship or escape from it, try as we may in our sinful attempts to run our own lives.

We are given the image of God in order that we may have dominion over the earth (v. 26). The dominion is the result of the image, not the content of it. But contrary to some criticisms that have been leveled by ecologists against this verse, our dominion or rule is always secondary to God's. Human beings never own the earth. "The earth is the Lord's, and the fullness thereof" (Psalm 24:1), and we are but God's stewards of his creation, his "passing guests," as Psalm 39:12 so beautifully puts it. In our care of the earth, we are responsible to God, and our existence is to point to God's supreme rule. As Gerhard von Rad has put it, we are like those statues of themselves that Roman emperors used to spread around their empires in order to show that the territory belonged to them. So, analogously, God has placed us, his little images across the face of the earth to point to the fact that the earth is his. Indeed, even when we go to the moon, we are not claiming it as our territory. We are taking God's image to the moon to show it belongs to him.

It is a strange note in this text that God at first gives only plants for human food (v. 30). However, in Genesis 9:2-3, meat is added, as a fuller gift of God, and Paul, in Romans 14:1-3 describes the vegetarian as one of weaker faith.

God completes his initial creation on the seventh day (Genesis 2:2), and then he rests, thus setting aside the seventh day as one devoted to rest — a sanctified period that will then be encoded in the Ten Commandments (Exodus 20:8-11; Deuteronomy 5:12-15). We should note carefully that the seventh day is set aside, not as a

149

day of worship — there are many other passages that call us to worship — but rather the seventh day is a time of rest from labor, not only for us, but for animals and servants and even land that is to lie fallow in the seventh year. Thus, one day of rest in a week is intended as a gift of God's merciful grace. He gives us our labor. But he also gives us our rest.

Finally, and importantly, Genesis 1:31 states that "God saw everything that he had made, and behold, it was very good." No evil was laid on the world by God, and if there is wrong in the world, it did not come from the Creator. God did not create the disruptions and distortions of his good creation of which we read in the morning headlines. God created his world good. It is only in the following chapters of Genesis that we read that we human beings introduced evil into our world.

Proper 5

Genesis 12:1-9

This text in Genesis 12 is one of the most important passages in the Bible for it lays the foundation for all that follows after. It records the beginning of God's salvation history that finally finds its fulfillment in Jesus Christ.

The passage cannot be understood apart from the preface to it in Genesis 1-11, however. Certainly it portrays God breaking into human history about 1750 B.C., to call a man named Abraham out of his home in Haran in upper Mesopotamia. But the question is: Why? Why was it necessary for God to speak his word into time and to give a promise to a nomadic semite?

The answer is found in what precedes this text. Genesis 1-11 tells the story of how all of us have walked in relation to our God. "Adam" is the Hebrew word for humankind, and so Genesis 1-11 is our story. It says that God created us and all things good. But in our attempt to run our own lives and to be our own gods and goddesses, we have rebelled against God's lordship (Genesis 3). The result is that we corrupted all of God's good gifts. We have distorted our intimate communion of love and fellowship with God (Genesis 3:8-10), corrupted the mutual communion of wife with husband (Genesis 3:7, 16), turned brother against brother (Genesis 4:1-16), and peoples against peoples (Genesis 4:23-24), until the earth is now full of wickedness that grieves God to his heart (Genesis 6:5-6). We destroy the loveliness and fecundity of nature (Genesis 3:17-19; 4:12), and in our proud search for power and security, make it impossible for nations to understand and get along with one another (Genesis 11:1-9). The result is that we live under God's sentence of death, for "the wages of sin is death."

But God has no pleasure in the death of anyone, and so with Abraham, he begins an actual history of salvation that will overcome all of the effects of our cursed rebellion against him, and that will restore his creation to the goodness he intended for it from the beginning.

To Abraham, God gives a threefold promise: "I will make of you a great nation," that is, God will make a new community of Abraham's many descendants, to replace the community that humankind has destroyed; "To your descendants I will give this land" that will flow with milk and honey, to replace the paradise that all of us have lost; "By you all the families of the earth shall be blessed," to turn the curse upon sin into the blessing and fullness of life that comes from God. And in Genesis 17:7, God adds one more promise: "I will establish my covenant between me and you and your descendants" to restore the relationship that we, in our rebellion against the Lord, have broken. The call of Abraham is the answer to human sin and the beginning of God's work of saving us all.

In the immediate context of our text, humankind wanted to make a name for itself (Genesis 11:4), but God will make Abraham's name great (12:2). Sarai was barren (11:30), but God will give her many descendants (12:2).

Genesis 12:1-9 records God's great reversal — the reversal of the history of sin, to replace it with the history of his salvation. God promises, and he always keeps his promise. And his saving work finally finds its consummation in our Lord Christ, who overcomes our sentence of death, restores us to communion with the Father, begins a universal community called the Christian Church, and is the source of blessing for all the families of the earth.

Lutheran Option: Hosea 5:15 — 6:6

Unfortunately, Hosea 5:15 should not be connected with 6:1-6. The word "saying" is missing in the Hebrew, and has only been added from the Septuagint. Originally the passages were not joined. If they do fit together, then what follows in 6:1-3 is a confession of guilt. But obviously, 6:1-3 is no such thing, as is evident from God's reply to the people's words in 6:4-6. Rather, 6:1-3 records Israel's phony repentance and belief that God will forgive her, no matter what she has done.

152

There is no doubt that Israel is in a jam. She is being engulfed by the Assyrian Empire (cf. 5:8-14), and so she has been summoned to a fast of repentance, in which she will plead for God to deliver her. She still has enough faith to know that Assyria is the "rod" of God's anger (cf. Isaiah 10:5), and that God is the only one who can rescue her.

And she is quite confident that God will do so. Israel in this eighth century B.C. time is very much like all of us. God has "torn" her, she believes (5:14), and so he will "heal" her (6:1). God has wounded her (5:13), and so he will bandage her up (6:2). God has become for Israel, as he often has become for us, simply a servant to take care of her needs — always forgiving, always loving, never judgmental, overlooking any defiance of his will. Indeed, he is just like one of those nature gods that the Canaanites — and often we — worship, Israel thinks — treating her gently like the spring rains that water the earth, demanding nothing in return. It is indicative of the Israelite's hollow repentance that their words in this passage are spoken not to God in prayer, but only to one another. Let's go find good ole god, is the tone, and he will deliver us from our difficulties.

But God has withdrawn from Israel to his place (5:15), and he cannot so easily be summoned to our aid. That is a sobering thought that we need to keep in mind. To be sure, God does not answer Israel's nonchalant devotion in wrath. Rather, he searches his mind and love for some way to save his unfaithful people, as he always searches for some way to save us. "What shall I do with you, O Ephraim?" (6:4) — the question of a loving Father to his disobedient child (cf. 11:1). Israel thinks she loves God, but her love is so ephemeral, disappearing at a moment's notice like dew dried up by the sun, as our love for God so easily dries up and disappears.

God has tried to correct his people, as he always tries to correct us. He has sent them prophets to issue his judgments upon Israel, just as the Word of God, if we study it carefully, always speaks God's judgments upon our disobedient lives. For what is the cross of Christ but the clear indication that sin, our sin, leads to death?

153

God does not disdain our offerings to him, our money given to his church, our service rendered in his name, our worship carried out every Sunday morning. But the question from our text is: Are our hearts involved in those offerings? Are we giving and serving and worshiping in sincere and heartfelt commitment to our Lord? For our text makes it very clear that above all else, God desires covenant love that cleaves to him like a faithful wife to her husband, or like an adoring son to his father. He wants our true knowledge of him, gained through Bible study and constant prayer every day, so we know the Lord we are worshiping. He wants *us* — heart, soul, mind, and strength, responding in love to his love, and committing ourselves to his lordship, above all other loyalties. Then, though we often fail, good Christians, we can truly say in all our difficulties, "Come, let us return to the Lord," and the Lord will reply to us, "Come!"

Proper 6

Genesis 18:1-15

In our Old Testament lesson last Sunday, we heard God promise to Abraham that he would be the forbear of a "great nation," of many descendants. Now in our text for the morning we find God beginning to work out his fulfillment of that promise by granting to Abraham and Sarah, his wife, the birth of a son, who will begin the line of descendants. God's promise is being effected in the sphere of actual history.

There are three versions in Genesis of the promise of a son to Abraham and Sarah. The first, from the source we call the Elohist, is found in Genesis 15:1-6. The second, from the priestly source, is in Genesis 17:15-21. The third, from the Yahwist of the tenth century B.C., forms our text for the morning. Those who edited the final form of our Bible kept all three versions of the promise, side by side, because, like the three Synoptic Gospels, all three have their own emphases and contribute to our understanding of God.

The author of our passage is noted for the vivid, earthly details of his accounts, and indeed, we have a very human picture given to us. The migrating semite, Abraham, is sitting at noontime before the door of his tent beside the oak trees of Mamre in the southern part of Palestine. Without warning and without any notice of where they come from, three men who are not identified, suddenly stand before the patriarch. Abraham is startled, but he is also a proper oriental host, who manifests his piety by his hospitality. He therefore welcomes the strangers with a bow, has his servant wash their feet, and then hastens to bid Sarah to prepare a cake, while he himself runs to fetch an expensive calf from his herd to be cooked for the visitors. There is great emphasis in the text on the quickness with which Abraham puts together the meal. Moreover, Abraham does not eat with the strangers, but stands by them, ready to fulfill any of their further wants.

155

Then comes the shocker in the text. One of the strangers asks, "Where is Sarah your wife?" A total stranger is not only asking about Abraham's wife, but even knows Sarah's name! And by that question we are alerted to the fact that the three men are more than just travelers through the desert. Indeed, we are then told in verse 10 that it is the Lord speaking to Abraham. "I will surely return to you in the spring, and Sarah your wife shall have a son."

We were never told earlier whether Abraham believed the promises of God to him. Certainly he left everything behind and started out for the land God would show him. But judging from the accounts in Genesis 15:2-3 and 17:17-18, Abraham did not believe that he would have a son from whom would come many descendants. After all, he and Sarah were both well past the age of childbearing (cf. 17:17). It is Sarah's disbelief that is highlighted in our text, however. She has been standing behind the tent flap, listening in on the conversation of the strangers with Abraham. And when she hears the promise of a son, she laughs, "Yizhach!" But that is Isaac's name that forever after signifies the fact that Sarah did not believe the Lord's promise.

It was not because of their great faith or piety or anything that they had done that Abraham and Sarah became the bearers of God's promise, any more than it is our great faith that prompts the Lord to work through us. Nevertheless, God is working his purpose out through each of our lives. Despite our sin, our unfaithfulness, our disbelief, God is gracious, and keeps his promises, and sometimes uses even us to move all history toward the coming of his kingdom on earth.

Lutheran Option: Exodus 19:2-8a

The Israelites have been delivered by the Lord from slavery in Egypt and are now trekking through the wilderness. After three arduous months of hiking, they encamp at the foot of Mount Sinai in the Arabian peninsula, and there they learn the purpose of their lives and of their deliverance.

Moses ascends Mount Sinai and God gives him words to set a choice before the Israelites. They have seen God's redemption of them; God has "bought them back" out of slavery, which is the meaning of redemption (cf. Leviticus 25:47-52). They have experienced God's love and mercy toward them. Now they are asked to respond. If they will enter into covenant with their God and keep the covenant, God will make them his "kingdom of priests and a holy nation." God has already chosen them as his people by delivering them in the exodus. But now he asks Israel if she will serve his purpose.

God wants the Israelites to be his "kingdom of priests." Here we find the first mention in the Bible of the priesthood of all believers. A priest is one who mediates between God and human beings, teaching the will and character of God to the people. So Israel is being asked to spread the knowledge of God in the earth. God also wants the Israelites to be his "holy nation." He is not saying that they should be morally perfect, although that is much to be desired. Rather, "to be holy," throughout the scriptures, is to be "set apart" for God's purposes. So God is asking Israel to be his "set-apart" people, his *'am segullah*, his "peculiar treasure" as the KJV has it, through whom God can work out his purpose in the world. And Israel, of her own free choice, agrees. "All that the Lord has spoken we will do" (v. 8). That is the purpose for which Israel has been redeemed — to be God's servant people.

We Christians in the church have also been redeemed, have we not — set free from our slavery to sin and death. Therefore, the same words that God spoke to Israel are spoken also to us in the New Testament. "You are a chosen race, a royal priesthood, a holy nation, God's own people" (1 Peter 2:9). There in a few words is described the nature of the church. Then the passage continues and gives us our reason for existence: "that you may declare the wonderful deeds of him who called you out of darkness into his marvelous light. Once you were no people but now you are God's people; once you had not received mercy but now you have received mercy" (1 Peter 2:9-10).

Now we know the purpose of our lives in the church, good Christians. As God's "royal priesthood," we are to mediate the

157

knowledge of God to all the world by telling of the wonderful deeds of God, not only in our own lives, but through all of the sacred history recorded for us in the Bible. For as God's "holy nation," we are set apart and made special to serve God's purpose in the world. We do not belong to ourselves any more, and we do not belong simply to our families or to some group in society. No. Now we belong to God, and the purpose for our lives is to serve his ongoing work of saving his world. Your life and mine, all of our lives, have meaning in that marvelous status and activity to which we have been called by our Lord.

Proper 7

Genesis 21:8-21

God has a way of humbling our pride. We consider ourselves in the Christian Church to be participants in the covenant people, chosen by God through Jesus Christ, to be the wild branches grafted into the root of Israel (cf. Romans 11:17-24), and thus heirs of all of the promises that God gave to Israel (cf. Galatians 4:4-7). As we heard last week, we are a special people, a kingdom of priests, and a holy nation. And that's pretty great. But lest we think we are better than anyone else, we encounter this story about Hagar and her son, Ishmael, in our Old Testament text for the morning.

As the story goes, Isaac has been born to Sarah and Abraham in their old age (Genesis 21:1-8), to begin the fulfillment of God's promise to them that they will be the forebears of many descendants. When Isaac is weaned from his mother, at about the age of three, there is great celebration.

But there is another child present in Abraham's camp who is also a descendant of Abraham — Ishmael, the son of Abraham's slave woman Hagar. Abraham fathered Ishmael, in accordance with the law, when it was thought that Sarah was barren (cf. Genesis 16:3-4). So Ishmael is the firstborn of Abraham. But he is not the child of the promise. Isaac is.

The two boys — Ishmael and Isaac — play together, as children will, and when Sarah sees them, fear fills her heart. She is afraid that Ishmael, whose name is not given in this account, will become Abraham's heir instead of Isaac. She therefore orders Abraham to get rid of the slave woman and child. Actually, by custom, that is Sarah's right, but Abraham has fatherly love for Ishmael, as well as for Isaac, and he does not want to accede to Sarah's jealous wish. (Contrast this attitude with Abraham's indifference in the parallel story in Genesis 16:1-14.) God, however, speaks to Abraham and tells him to banish Hagar and her son, because God has other plans for them. Ishmael too will become the forbear of a nation, while Isaac will be Abraham's heir and the bearer of the promise.

In other words, as he does so often, God is here working out the fulfillment of his promise in circumstances that seem to us quite wrong. God uses even the jealousy and hatred and fear in the human heart to accomplish his purpose (cf. Genesis 45:4-8). He will not be deterred!

But God does not desert Hagar and Ishmael either. The Lord is, above all else, a Lord of love. Hagar is sent away from the camp in the early morning with only the most meager supply of food and water. And once those are gone and her child is crying with thirst, she places Ishmael under a bush and goes a distance away, because she cannot stand to see him die. But "Ishmael" means "God hears." And God hears the voice of the child. An angel, who represents God, opens Hagar's eyes to see a well of water, and Hagar is promised that her son will not die, but will become the father of a great nation. And from that time on, says our text, God is with Ishmael (v. 20). Indeed, Ishmael becomes the forbear of those nomads, who had herds of cattle, who wandered the fringes of settlements in the southern part of Palestine.

We are members of God's covenant people, yes. But that does not mean that God loves and favors us any more than he loves other people, of whatever race or status. God cares for all folk, and so we are to care for them, too. In fact, the status to which we are called is to be a servant people to the rest of humanity.

Lutheran Option: Jeremiah 20:7-13

This passage is one of those prayers that are known as Jeremiah's "confessions." We see the prophet in desperate straits, crying out and, in fact, accusing God of deceiving (literally, "seducing") him. God commanded Jeremiah to proclaim judgment on his sinful people in the form of attack and destruction by the armies of Babylonia. But the judgment has not come. Between the years of 604-601 B.C., Babylonia does not appear, and as a result, Jeremiah has become a laughingstock of his compatriots. "Where is the Word of the Lord?" they hoot. "Let it come!" (Jeremiah 17:15). They accuse Jeremiah of being a false prophet, which can lead to the death penalty (20:10). They curse him and openly oppose him (15:10), mimic his words (20:10; cf. v. 3) and even once subject him to beating, arrest, and a night in the stocks, where every passerby can hit him and spit on him (20:1-2). The prophet therefore accuses God of betraying him. We see from this prophet that prayer need not take the form of pious phrases, but can be uttered in open frankness and realism.

Jeremiah tries to escape his dreadful situation by shutting up God's word inside of him and not speaking, but the word is too powerful for him. It becomes, says the prophet, like a burning fire, shut up in his bones, and he cannot help but proclaim it (v. 9). The Word of God is more powerful than all human will and desire. And we see here the suffering that bearers of that word must sometimes undergo as God's servants.

This prayer has the form of what we call a "lament" in the Old Testament, a form found frequently in the Psalms (cf. Psalm 3, 5, 6, etc.). And as do most of the laments, this one switches from accusation and complaint to trust and assurance of God's help. God is with him, says the prophet, like a "dread warrior" (v. 11). That is not a term that we often use of God. But God is a warrior against sin throughout the Bible, and our prophet knows deep down in his soul that God is warring against Judah's sin. In prophetic vision, he has seen that warfare (cf. e.g. 4:5-8, 19-21, 29-31). And so Jeremiah knows he has been proclaiming a true word of judgment, and he realizes that, in the end, his persecutors will be shown wrong and shamed.

We should notice very carefully, however, that Jeremiah does not take vengeance into his own hands against his opponents and persecutors. Rather, he turns his case over to the Lord. "O Lord ... let me see *thy* vengeance upon them, for to thee have I committed my cause." Everything is left in God's hands, and Jeremiah can get on with the fearsome task to which his Lord has called him. God, in his time, will work out his own purpose. Jeremiah's calling is simply to be the servant of that purpose.

161

Jeremiah's words did prove true, of course. That is the reason we have his words preserved for us in the Old Testament — because his words were fulfilled by God, thus vindicating Jeremiah's prophetic calling. To be sure, Jeremiah suffered for that calling. When God called him in his youth to be a prophet, he was told that he would be set against the whole land (1:18), and that was true most of his life. But anyone who resolves in faith to be a servant for the Lord necessarily takes on a role that contradicts most of the ways of a sinful society. It often is not easy to be a Christian. Nevertheless, our final assurance is that God is with us and that his powerful Word and saving purpose will prevail against all the enemies opposed to them.

Proper 8

Genesis 22:1-14

We must not water down this text. It has often been said that coming from a pagan Mesopotamia background, Abraham mistakenly believed that God wanted him to sacrifice Isaac. And once even the wife of Martin Luther objected, "Martin, I don't believe God would ask anyone to sacrifice his only son." But the text is to be taken quite seriously. "God tested Abraham." And that test comes after "these things." Well, what things? Certainly Abraham's initial doubt that God could give him a son in his old age, and Abraham's admonition to the Lord to do right, in chapter 19, and his need to be corrected by God in the story of Hagar and Ishmael. Abraham's faith is on the line in this story in Genesis 22, and the question is: Will he pass the test?

The emotional depth of this story can only be sensed by reading it slowly and aloud, with emphasis on the repetitions. Repeatedly we find "your son," "his son," "my father," "they went both of them together." The language is sparse and unsentimental, but the repetitions leave no doubt of the love between the innocent son and his anguished father. Not a word is said about Sarah or about how Abraham and Isaac feel, but we cannot read the story carefully and not know how they feel.

Yet, Abraham in obedience to God's command, rises early and saddles his ass, and taking two of his servants and a bundle of wood for the burnt offering, sets out with his son, his only son Isaac, to go to the land of Moriah where there is a mountain of sacrifice. In tenderness up to the end, Abraham himself carries the fire and the knife, lest the young boy hurt himself with them. And his faith, in answer to Isaac's wondering question is, "God himself will provide the lamb for a burnt offering, my son."

The sacrifice is not carried out, because God provides a word of halt and a substituting ram, and Abraham is shown to have passed the test of his faith. The question was: Whom does Abraham trust? He has been granted the gift of Isaac in fulfillment of God's promise. But now does he trust the gift and cling to Isaac, in defiance of God, or does he trust the Giver? Does he trust that God knows what he is doing and is keeping his promise of descendants? Because Abraham finally trusts God, the promise of the Lord to him is renewed (cf. Genesis 12:1-3), and Abraham becomes the progenitor of all of the covenant people, including you and me.

That same test of trust was what our Lord faced too in the Garden of Gethsemane. As the cross lay before him, did he trust that his Father knew what he was doing in asking his sacrifice? When Martin Luther's wife objected to God's demand that Abraham sacrifice his only son, Luther replied, "But, Katie, God did." And the story of the sacrifice of Jesus is very similar to this one in Genesis. Legend has it that Moriah became the site of Jerusalem. And like Isaac, Jesus journeyed to Moriah in the company of his Father. But there is little there too that the Father and Son say to one another on the journey — only that prayer in the garden, "Father, if it be possible, let this cup pass from me." The answer Jesus receives is the same as Isaac's: "The sacrifice must be carried out, my Son." Like Isaac, Jesus carries the wood up the hill, until he is relieved of the burden by Simon of Cyrene. Like Isaac, Jesus is laid out upon the wood. And as the knife was raised above Isaac, so the hammer is raised above Jesus. But there is no substituting ram to save our Lord from the awful death, no rescuing Elijah, no miraculous descent from the torture of the cross.

Our question to both Genesis 22 and to the story of the crucifixion is: Why? And the answer is the same in both instances. God is carrying out his purpose of saving his world. Through Abraham's faith, God can continue his work of salvation with Israel. And with Christ's death and resurrection, God can bring the story to its climax, overcoming by the cross and empty tomb our sin and our death.

Lutheran Option: Jeremiah 28:5-9

The setting of this text is in Jerusalem, shortly after 597 B.C., when the armies of Babylonia have conquered Jerusalem and carried off most of its leaders, artisans, warriors, and upper class to exile in Babylonia, along with an enormous booty and the temple treasures. The davidic king Jehoichin has been replaced on the throne by the puppet Zedekiah, Judah's territory has been greatly reduced, and she is left with virtually no political leaders or economic resources. Intrigue and insurrection against the Babylonian yoke are rife in the capital city, however, fed by a pro-Egyptian party, and by popular prophets.

One of those prophets is Hananiah, who is telling the people that within two years, Babylonia will be defeated and all of the exiles and treasures will be returned to Judah (Jeremiah 28:1-4). The prophet Jeremiah, on the other hand, knows that the exile is God's judgment on Judah's sinful ways and that the exile will be long. Therefore Jeremiah writes a letter to the exiles in Babylonia, urging them to settle down there, to build houses and plant gardens, to intermarry with the foreigners, and even to pray for Babylonia, for God can be found in Babylonia as well as in Jerusalem (Jeremiah 29:1-14). To symbolize the fact that the Judeans should submit to Babylonia and not revolt, Jeremiah is commanded to wear a wooden yoke on his neck (Jeremiah 27:1-12). Hananiah, however, breaks the yoke, whereupon Jeremiah replaces it with a yoke of iron (28:10-17).

Two emphases run through our text. First is the refusal of the prophet Hananiah and of the Judeans to admit their sin and thus to understand their defeat by Babylonia as the judgment of God. That is a familiar view among us, is it not, to refuse to see any calamity as God's judgment on our sin? Indeed, it is very hard for us even to admit that we have done wrong. Right and wrong are relative terms these days, and when we or others commit wrong, we often rationalize it as a mistake or a "goof," or as the result of circumstances at the time. Maybe we or the perpetrator were tired, or had been drinking or were on drugs. Maybe someone else was a bad influence, or our parents didn't raise us right. Maybe the poor environment was the cause, and there should be a massive government spending program to correct that. We are not to blame. It's someone else's responsibility, and of course, God won't judge us for that. But we daily experience the judgment of God in our wrecked marriages, our crime-ridden cities, our children gone awry, our sex-saturated society. We are responsible to God for what we do, as Judah was responsible. And we cannot escape the effects of that.

The second emphasis of our text rises from the first and concerns the validity of the Word of God. Hananiah has been prophesying peace, harmony, good to the people, and Jeremiah is willing to say that perhaps Hananiah is correct. But there is a test of that word of prophecy: Does it come to pass? Is that what the Judeans are going to receive? The implication of course is that the true Word of God is always fulfilled, and so the Judeans can tell the difference between the true and the false prophet by their fruits (cf. Matthew 7:16).

Jeremiah knows that the false prophets through the years have been preaching, "peace, peace," when there is no peace with God (Jeremiah 6:14; 8:11). And he also knows that the people are responsible to God for their sins. Thus the text stands as a warning to all of us to "beware of false prophets, who come to (us) in sheep's clothing" (Matthew 7:15). Beware of those who tell you that you can have the good life, success, happiness from God without the necessity of confessing or even acknowledging your sins and your responsibility to God for them. A lot of the religious messages we hear these days from the false prophets of our time are designed just to make us feel good about ourselves. But does God feel good about you and what you do? That is the question to ask.

Proper 9

Genesis 24:34-38, 42-49, 58-67

God has promised Abraham that he will be the forebear of many descendants. To begin to fulfill that promise, God has granted the aged Abraham and Sarah a son, Isaac. That is the context of this story that must never be forgotten.

But now Isaac is grown to marriageable age and Abraham must find a suitable wife for him, as was the custom. Abraham is probably at Hebron in this story, but Isaac must not be wed to a Canaanite woman who worships the foreign fertility gods of the region. Abraham therefore binds his servant (a steward here) by an oath (24:1-9) to seek out a woman from Abraham's own clan in Haran in upper Mesopotamia, from which Abraham had migrated.

The emphasis of the story is on the hidden guidance of God. The verses of our passage repeat the account of the events that take place in verses 10-33, and at every point, God's influence determines what happens. Abraham's wealth has been a gift from God (v. 35). God's angel accompanies the servant and "prospers" his way (v. 40). God gives heed to the prayer of the servant (vv. 42-44) and prompts Rebekah's actions to be the sign that identifies her as God's appointed wife for Isaac (vv. 42-46).

Once Rebekah is identified as the chosen wife, every character in the story acknowledges that God's has been the guiding hand — the servant (v. 48); Laban, Rebekah's brother, and her father Bethuel (v. 50); by implication, Rebekah in her willingness to depart immediately for Canaan rather than to wait the accustomed ten days (vv. 56-59); and finally Isaac who, upon hearing the servant's account of the journey, immediately takes Rebekah as his wife (vv. 66-67). This is not merely a charming human story, but a testimony to the specific acts of God as he works to fulfill his promise. Thus does the God of the Bible work his hidden will in the lives of his chosen people.

The character of Rebekah is revealed. She is not only beautiful (v. 16), but unselfish. To water the servant's camels, she repeatedly must climb down stairs to the hole from which the spring flows, and then carry the heavy water jar back up and empty it into the watering trough beside the well. She also is pious, trusting that the servant is in fact following God's leading, and placing her future in his hands. And Rebekah is loving (v. 67), a wife who merits Jacob's love and gives him comfort after the death of his mother (v. 67).

Note that there is no thought here that a wife is simply property to be bought by a man — a common misconception about marriage in the Old Testament. Isaac pays the accustomed bride price with the jewels that the servant gives to Rebekah (v. 22) and to her mother and brother (v. 53), but this is a marriage of love, not of convenience or commerce. Many passages in the Old Testament hold marriage in high regard (cf. Genesis 2:23-25; 29:20; Malachi 2:14).

The blessing that Rebekah's family gives her as she departs forms an ironic touch to the story. They wish her multiple descendants (v. 60), but she is initially barren (Genesis 25:21), an obstacle to the fulfillment of the promise that God himself must overcome, in answer to Isaac's prayer. Throughout these patriarchal narratives God is the principal subject, as indeed, he is the principle actor throughout the scriptures and in our lives. God is continually at work to keep his word. We can count on it.

Lutheran Option: Zechariah 9:9-12

This passage which is often used in connection with Palm Sunday, but which also finds its place in this Pentecost season in connection with the latter part of the Gospel lesson of Matthew 11:25-29, is sometimes misinterpreted. The passage forms an announcement of the coming of the davidic messianic king to Jerusalem, and that which sermons often emphasize is the humility of that king. Thus, the reading is made to fit nicely with Matthew 11:29-30. But the error that is made is to say that the Messiah comes humbly because he is riding on a lowly beast of burden, on an ass. (One can even find choral songs and imaginative stories celebrating that fact.)

That which is not realized is that riding on an ass was not a sign of the Messiah's humility, but of his identity. Princes rode on asses, according to Judges (5:10; 10:4; 12:14), as did King David (2 Samuel 16:2). But most telling, it is promised in Genesis 49:10-11 that the Messiah would ride on that beast. Thus the Messiah can be recognized!

The promised messianic ruler is humble, however, because he is completely dependent on God. In verse 10 of our passage, it is not the Messiah who speaks, but God. And God is the one who will banish all weapons of war and enable the Messiah to establish a reunited Israel that will enjoy peace from the Reed Sea to the Mediterranean, and from the wilderness of Sinai to the Euphrates. In short, the Messiah will have his universal reign from the hand of God, as for example in Isaiah 11:1-9.

Similarly, verse 9 of our passage is translated in the RSV, for example, as "triumphant and victorious is he." But a better translation is "righteous and saved is he." Throughout the scriptures "righteousness" is the fulfillment of a relationship, and the Messiah will be righteous because he trusts God and rules as a king should rule (cf. Isaiah 11:3b-4a). He will protect the helpless and prosper the good and be like "the shadow of a mighty rock within a weary land" (Isaiah 32:2), but he will do such things because God will enable him to do them (cf. Psalm 72:1). Similarly, he will be "saved" from his enemies, because God will save him.

The Messiah is "humble" therefore, because his life and reign and abilities lie solely in God's hands, upon whom he is totally dependent for the success of his kingship and for the peace of his kingdom. He has no authority except that given him by God (cf. Psalm 110:1-5; 2:6-9). The picture is consonant with everything said about the Messiah in the Royal Psalms and in the prophetic writings.

That our Lord fulfilled this prophecy and was God's promised Messiah cannot be doubted. The New Testament affirms that fact

169

throughout its pages. But it also affirms this portrayal of the Messiah in Zechariah. Christ relies on his Father for everything. He does nothing on his own authority, speaks only the words given him by his Father, follows not his own will but that of his Father, and points always to the goodness and glory of God and not to his own. That is true humility, and our Lord is, indeed, as Matthew writes, "gentle and lowly in heart," who can give us "rest for (our) souls" when we "labor and are heavy laden."

Proper 10

Genesis 25:19-34

It may seem rather startling to read in verse 20 of this passage that Isaac is forty years old when he marries Rebekah. In the text of Genesis 24 that we looked at last Sunday, Isaac was just a young man of marriageable age, for whom his father Abraham was obliged to find a wife. The disparity in the accounts is due to the fact that we have two sources woven together here. Verses 19-20 of our text today come from the priestly source. Chapter 24 and 25:21-34 come from the Yahwist source, and the two sources differ in their chronologies. Perhaps this is an opportunity for the preacher to explain to the congregation that some of the contradictions in the scriptures are due to the interweaving of separate sources.

This text in chapter 25 forms an introduction to what follows in the Genesis narrative. Once again the background is the promise of many descendants, and this text serves to illumine why Jacob becomes the chosen one of the Lord and the bearer of the promise. It also reflects the lifestyles of the inhabitants of Palestine — the darker-skinned, somewhat scruffy hunters of the eastern and southern regions, the more civilized shepherds of Israel.

Always there seem to be obstacles to God's fulfillment of his promise. Rebekah, the beloved wife of Isaac, is barren, which was a matter of shame in ancient Israel. And according to the priestly writer, she is barren for twenty years (v. 26). But then the Yahwist story tells us that Isaac prays for his wife and she conceives (v. 21), which is an explicit notice here, as throughout the Bible, that all human life is created by God.

Rebekah's pregnancy, however, is difficult, and she thinks she cannot bear the stress and pain that it causes her. She, too, therefore, goes to a cult center and prays, inquiring of the priest there why she is in so much distress. The word of the Lord, conveyed to her by the priest, forms a prophecy of the future. She will bear twins, but the lastborn will rule over the firstborn. That word is then confirmed not only by the fact that Jacob grasps his brother's heel at birth and is therefore named "supplanter," but also by the name "Edom," signifying the "red" pottage for which Esau, the forbear of the Edomites, trades his birthright.

By right, as the firstborn, Esau should inherit the wealth and honor of his father Isaac. And it is to Esau that the dim-eyed and dying Isaac should later give his blessing (ch. 27), conveying all his goods and status. But Jacob is a "supplanter," Jacob is a cheat — a characteristic that marks him throughout his life — and he cheats his brother out of both the inheritance and the blessing. Esau swears to the transaction — the oath is necessary to insure it (v. 33) — simply because he is famished after a day of hunting. Physical hunger determines his actions, as physical desires often determine ours. And what Esau ends up with is not some delicious game, but a mess of cheap lentil pottage that he hastily gulps down.

The little notice that "Rebekah loved Jacob" (v. 28) will later be shown to be a love that saves Jacob's life (27:41-45). But perhaps the basic question that confronts us from this passage is why a man like Jacob — a supplanter, a deceiver of his brother, a cheat who will continue his cheating ways in his Uncle Laban's house (30:37-43) — should be the person chosen by God to inherit Isaac's goods and blessing and to bear the promise of the Lord. Jacob has taken advantage of his weaker brother Esau, and he is totally undeserving of any consideration or grace from the Lord.

So are we undeserving of God's care and mercy, are we not? We never deserved that cross on Golgotha and the forgiveness of our sins. We never deserved the promise of eternal life through Christ's resurrection. We never have deserved God's constant watch over us, his guidance every day, his comfort in sorrow, his strength in distress, even his gifts of sun and rain, and our daily bread. But God has lavished them all on us. And what is more he has chosen us, as he chose Jacob, to be his special people set apart for his purpose. We are elect, as Jacob was elect, through no deserving of our own. Surely, our response to that can only be overwhelming gratitude and a daily desire to walk in God's ways and to be his faithful covenant people.

Lutheran Option: Isaiah 55:10-13

The prophecies of Second Isaiah (Isaiah 40-55) begin and end with the proclamation that the Word of God will not and cannot fail. To the exiles in Babylonia sometime after 550 B.C., the prophet announces that all of God's past promises to Israel — of land, descendants, covenant communion, Davidic king, and blessing — will be gathered up and brought to fulfillment, because "the Word of our God will stand forever" (Isaiah 40:8). And here in our passage, that is reaffirmed. God tells us that the word "shall accomplish that which I purpose" (55:11). God's Word presses on through human history to accomplish God's goal.

Our usual understanding of the Word of God does not begin to encompass what the scriptures mean by those terms. We usually think of the Word of God as identical with the Bible ("the Word of God written"), or as a proclamation from the pulpit, or as teaching passed on, all of which just give us new understandings or new information about the Lord and human beings and the world.

But the biblical understanding of the Word of God is much more dynamic than that. Throughout the scriptures, the Word of God is understood as active, effective force, which brings about new situations, and which influences and shapes the course of history, until that which the word says is brought to pass. To give a simple illustration, in Genesis 1, God says, "Let their be light," and light is created (Genesis 1:3) — a new situation comes into being.

In our text, therefore, God speaks of this active nature of his Word. Just as the rain and snow come down from heaven and cause seeds to sprout and grow, so God's word *causes* events. It does that of which it speaks. The word works until it is fulfilled. So Bible and biblical sermon not only convey information. Much more, they communicate the powerful Word of God that works to transform human lives. As Paul says, when Christ is preached and faith in him is aroused, that Word of God incarnate makes a "new creation. The old has passed away, behold the new has come" (2 Corinthians 5:17). Our past is done away; our sins are forgiven; and we are

173

made into new persons who, by Christ at work in us, are able to do his will.

God speaks many words to us through Bible and sermon and sacrament. And one of those words is, "I am the resurrection and the life; he who believes in me, though he die, yet shall he live" (John 11:23). And that Word of God will work in our lives, good Christians, until we are, indeed, granted eternal life.

Proper 11

Genesis 28:10-19a

Jacob is on a journey from Hebron to Haran, Abraham's original home in northern Mesopotamia. In the context, two different reasons are given for the journey. According to the Yahwist account in Genesis 27:41-45, Jacob is fleeing to save his life from the wrath of his brother Esau. In the priestly account of Genesis 27:46—28:1-5, Jacob journeys to find a wife from his own clan. Both reasons may be involved, because God's purpose works its way through all sorts of motivations. Before Jacob takes leave of his father Isaac, however, Isaac blesses Jacob with the wish that Jacob may become the bearer of God's promise (28:3-4). Our text for the morning tells how that comes about.

A day's journey out, Jacob camps for the night at a place originally called Luz. As he sleeps, pillowing his head with a stone (undoubtedly covered with his cloak), he has a dream of a ladder — or more properly, a stepped ramp — reaching up into heaven, with angels descending and ascending on the ramp. And above the top end of the ramp, the Lord stands and addresses Jacob.

God identifies himself as the same God who spoke to Abraham and to Isaac, and then he gives to Jacob the same promise that he gave to Abraham (cf. Genesis 12:1-3). Jacob will have many descendants; God will give them a land to call their own; and through them, God will bring his blessing on all the families of the earth (28:13-14). In short, through Jacob and his descendants God will continue his work of restoring his world to the goodness that he intended for it in the beginning. God's plan is continuing to be worked out in history.

An additional promise to Jacob personally follows, however. God will protect Jacob and bring him back to Canaan, and God will never leave Jacob until all that God has promised him is fulfilled (v. 15). Jacob is journeying under the protection and guidance of a divine guarantee. That is the same assurance that our Lord gave to us when he promised, "Lo, I am with you always, to the close of the age" (Matthew 28:20). And it is the basis of the same confidence that Paul expressed to the Philippians, "I am sure that he who began a good work in you will bring it to completion in the day (i.e. the second coming) of Jesus Christ" (Philippians 1:6). Our lives are not lonely battles and aimless excursions through the valleys and heights of our everydays, but guided and watched over by the Lord who is working out his purpose through us.

Jacob is awestruck when he wakes, realizing that he has encountered God at the meeting place of heaven and earth (vv. 16-17). As a result, he sets his stone pillow up as an altar and names the site, "Beth-el," "the house of God" (vv. 18-19), marking it forever after as a holy place.

These last four verses, 16-19, have often been misused in sermons and meditations and at summer camp sites. Some worship leader will tell us that a church building or some structure or outdoor setting is "the house of God" with God present there. And contrary to the text, and indeed the scriptures as a whole, God then is understood as available anywhere at any time according to our word (contra Deuteronomy 12:5; Isaiah 55:6). But Jacob has been privy to the place where heaven meets earth, and there is only one location of that meeting place for us — in Jesus Christ. In him, we encounter the Father, and only through him (John 14:6). And it is only because Christ has promised to be with two or three gathered together in his name (Matthew 18:20) that we can say our church building or some other worship location is the place where we meet God. We cannot command God's gracious presence, but nevertheless, he grants himself to us in his Son.

Lutheran Option: Isaiah 44:6-8

Here in the strongest terms we encounter the monotheism of the Old Testament. There is no other God besides the God revealed to us through the witnesses preserved for us in the scriptures. God is the first and the last (v. 6), the Alpha and the Omega (cf. Revelation 1:8), the One at the beginning and at the end of human time and history, the eternal Lord, before and after all things (cf. Psalm 90:1-2). It is in Second Isaiah (Isaiah 40-55), spoken to exiles in Babylonia who were surrounded by foreign deities, that we find the strongest statements in the Old Testament of the sole Godhead of the Lord.

But on what basis does the prophet Second Isaiah proclaim that fact? On two bases of history. First of all, God has had the power to rule over nature and empire and other gods in order to deliver his people Israel from slavery in Egypt. He was not thwarted by the gods of Egypt or by the power of a Pharaoh or by the waters of the Reed Sea. He "redeemed" his people — bought them back from their servitude (cf. Leviticus 25:47-49), which is the meaning of redemption. And God became their King and their Redeemer (Isaiah 44:6; cf. 6:1; 43:15, et al.).

Second, God is the One who rules over all of history. He can tell what is coming in the future, because he holds the future in his hand. He has a plan that he is working out over all the span of time, and he therefore knows what the future holds and what the end will be (Isaiah 44:7). No other religion or deity in the world has a purpose that over-arches the entire human story. Indeed, most religions of the world try to escape out of human history. But the Lord God of Israel and of Jesus Christ has that purpose, and he is day by day, month by month, year by year, century by century accomplishing it.

The proclamation of verse 8 can therefore also be spoken to us, good Christians. "Fear not, nor be afraid!" For we too have been redeemed from our slavery to sin and death, have we not — redeemed by the cross and resurrection of Jesus Christ? And we too have been told by our Lord what the end of human history will be — the Kingdom of God come on earth even as it is in heaven. Therefore, we too need not fear either things present or things to come, either life or death, principalities or powers, or anything in all creation, because we know — we know with certain joy — that God rules over our lives and universe and is directing them toward his glad conclusion. What is the world coming to? It is coming to Christ, when every knee will bow to him and every tongue confess, that he is Lord of all, to the glory of God the Father (Philippians 2:10-11; cf. Isaiah 45:23).

Proper 12

Genesis 29:15-28

We find before us a very worldly story of love and deceit on the part of two very worldly men. All through these stories of Jacob and Laban we find two scoundrels who seem bent on trying to outdo the other in trickery. Far from dealing with only some ethereal, spiritual realm, the Bible throughout deals with the grubbiness of human life as it is actually lived. And it is in the middle of that sordidness, with its power-plays and pettiness, that the scriptures find God at work.

Jacob has fled toward his Uncle Laban's house in Mesopotamia to escape the wrath of his brother Esau, whom Jacob has cheated out of his birthright and blessing as the firstborn of Isaac. As Jacob nears Haran, he encounters a group of shepherds keeping their sheep, who point out Rachel, Laban's daughter, to him. It apparently is love at first sight. Rachel is "beautiful and lovely" (v. 17) and Jacob knows that he must make her his wife.

Because Jacob is going to stay with Laban for awhile and work for him, Laban asks what wages Jacob requires. Jacob, in an extravaganza of love, says that he will work for Laban for seven years if Laban will consent for Rachel to marry him (v. 18).

The clinker in the story is that Laban has two daughters, Leah, which means "cow," and who has "weak" eyes — that is, her eyes are not dark and lustrous, but pale and shading toward blue. She apparently is not very attractive, but she is the older of the two sisters (vv. 16-17). Rachel, which means "ewe," on the other hand is lovely, and because Jacob loves her so much, the seven years that he works to obtain her seem to him like a few days (v. 20). His is definitely a relationship of deepest love with Rachel, not a commercial arrangement.

It is not proper for the younger daughter to marry prior to the older, however, and so when the wedding night comes, Laban substitutes a heavily-veiled Leah for Rachel in the wedding tent. Imagine Jacob's shock the next morning, after the marriage has been consummated, when he awakes and "behold, it is Leah" (v. 25). Jacob is furious, as well he might be. But Laban promises him that if he will go along with the week of wedding festivities and then work seven more years, he may have Rachel as a wife also at the end of the festivities. So Jacob gets his heart's desire and Rachel is his at the end of the seven days, but he must continue to work for seven years as the bridal price paid for her (vv. 26-30).

It is not a happy arrangement. Jacob hates Leah and loves Rachel, but Rachel is barren, while the Lord in mercy opens Leah's womb. God, it seems, always favors the despised, the outcast, and the helpless. And it is Leah who becomes the mother of the for-bears of four of the tribes of Israel — Reuben, Simeon, Levi, and Judah. With the birth of each son, poor Leah hopes, apparently in vain, that the child will cause Jacob to love her too (vv. 31-39). We never hear that such love is given, however, and indeed, the narrator's interest is entirely centered on the sons who are born.

What is such a secular story doing in the Bible? Other than revealing to us the mercy of God toward one despised, does it say anything to us about the working of the Lord? Well, yes, it does, because from Leah, the ugly and hated wife, later comes forth David from the tribe of Judah and Moses from the tribe of Levi. God has used, as he so often does, a seemingly distasteful situation to continue to further his purpose for his people Israel. God takes the most unlikely situation and turns it into a cause of blessing. Here he uses Laban's deceit, and Jacob's love, and Leah's pitiful longing to set the stage for the future deliverance of his people from slavery under Moses and for the coming rule over his people of their greatest king, David. Only a God whose purpose spans all time can do such deeds.

Perhaps that is a revelation to us of the fact that even what seems to us at the time to be the most dreadful situation may be an integral part of the ongoing purpose of God that he is working out through our lives. While we know only the moment, God knows the outcome, and he uses even our most desperate moments to work out his loving purpose.

Lutheran Option: 1 Kings 3:5-12

With this text we enter into the world of Deuteronomic theology. It has long been the view of scholars that everything in the books of Judges through 2 Kings has been edited about 550 B.C. by those who are known as the Deuteronomic editors. Typical of those editors in our text is the high estimation of the faithful kingship of David (v. 6) and of the initial wisdom of Solomon, around whose name many Wisdom traditions clustered.

Most important for our purposes, however, is the Deuteronomic view of the Davidic kingship that is found in Deuteronomy 17:14-20. The preacher should read that passage and note that its main requirement for a good king is that he not accumulate for himself the trappings of other oriental monarchs (Deuteronomy 17:16-17), but that he faithfully follow the Deuteronomic covenant law, walking in God's ways, cleaving to God, and loving the Lord with all his heart and mind and strength.

We are told immediately, therefore, in our text that Solomon loved the Lord and walked in the covenant statues, as did his father David (v. 3). Solomon does not yet worship only at Jerusalem, as Deuteronomy prescribes, because the temple has not yet been built (v. 4), but following our passage, Solomon does offer his thanksgiving sacrifice in that holy city (v. 15).

But in our passage, Solomon is granted a revelatory dream at the place of worship in Gibeon (vv. 5, 15) and because of his love for the Lord, is allowed to ask a gift of the Lord (v. 5). Rather than choosing long life or riches or military victories (cf. v. 11), Solomon asks for an understanding mind to discern between good and evil, to make judicial judgments rightly (which is the meaning of v. 11), and to have wisdom to rule his people. In short, Solomon chooses the pattern of kingship laid out by Deuteronomy. His request is framed in the most humble terms — three times he calls himself God's "servant" (vv. 7-9), and he further states that he does not know how "to go out and come in," which is a general expression for leadership. In short, Solomon's desire is to have the wisdom which will prosper the welfare of his people. He wants not his own glory, but that wisdom which will allow him faithfully to fulfill his covenant duties to God.

Because Solomon has chosen thus, God grants him also, as a free gift, riches and honor (v. 13) and long life, *if* Solomon will continue faithful to the covenant law (v. 14).

In the brief space allotted, we cannot discuss Solomon's subsequent disobedience (cf. 1 Kings 11). But because governments are ordained by God to promote right among the populace (cf. Romans 13), we can point to the ideal for rule that this passage sets before us. A ruler, a leader, a president, who is concerned primarily for the welfare of his people, and who wisely promotes that welfare by discerning between good and evil and by knowing what is right — surely in our day those are the qualities to look for in those whom we elect to govern us.

Proper 13

Genesis 32:22-31

At the command of God (Genesis 31:13), Jacob is returning to Canaan from Haran after twenty years of labor (cf. 31:14) for his Uncle Laban. He is returning a very rich man. He now has two wives and multiple children and servants and hundreds of goats and rams, camels and cows (cf. 32:14-15), many of which he has acquired by cheating Laban. He is returning as the same shrewd scoundrel that he has always been. Consequently, when he hears that his brother Esau is coming out to meet him with 400 picked men (32:6), he divides his herds in two and sends half of them ahead of him as a present for Esau, to appease his brother's wrath. At the same time, he sends his wives and maids and eleven children across the difficult ford of the Jabbok River in the dark of the night (32:22). And then Jacob, the cheat, the rich man is left with his own thoughts in the dark of the night beside the river.

Jacob, however, the bearer of God's promise, is not alone. He is suddenly attacked by some mysterious figure who wrestles with him until daybreak. We are not told who the figure is until verses 28 and 30 in our text, where it is said that Jacob has "striven with men and with God" and has "seen God face to face." In the wrestling, Jacob's thigh is put out of joint, and he limps away from his desperate encounter.

Much in this story seems exceedingly mysterious to us. For example, the strange figure tells Jacob to let him go before daybreak (v. 26). Lying behind the story, therefore, is the ancient belief that God is not to be seen by human beings. Similarly, the divine figure refuses to tell Jacob his name (v. 29), and again, that echoes the belief that to know a god's name is to be able to summon the deity to one's aid at will.

Most important, however, is the fact that in these ancient stories of the patriarchs, Israel saw herself. It is in this wrestling with

God that Jacob's name is changed to "Israel," meaning "he who strives with God," or "God strives." Not only Israel's forbear Jacob is the bearer of God's promise (cf. v. 12), but the whole people are the ones to whom God gives the promise of land and descendants and covenant, and the whole people are to be the medium of God's blessing on all the families of the earth. Like us members of God's new covenant, Israel of the old covenant is set apart for God's purpose of being his kingdom of priests and his holy nation (cf. Exodus 19:6; 1 Peter 2:9).

What, then, is this story telling us? First, it shows that our election by God costs us something. Jacob is wounded in his wrestling with God, and limps away toward his destination of the promised land. Israel — and we — are chosen by God, not for privilege but for service. And that election and that service cost us something. It is not easy to be a servant of God, either in Jacob's time, or in ours. Saint Paul could tell us that — look at the list of sufferings he has endured that he recounts in 2 Corinthians 11:23-33. But most of all, look at the cross, where we learn that God's battle with the sins of the world involves a crucifixion. If we want to be God's people, then we take up a cross. We die to ourselves, that Christ may live in us and make us new people. And that brings with it sometimes scorn from society, even sometimes persecution, as Christians around our world could testify to us.

Second, this story about Jacob's wrestling tells us that it is the persistence of our faith that wins the battle to which God subjects us. Jacob cries out in this story to his divine assailant, "I will not let you go unless you bless me" (v. 26). Sometimes we have not the foggiest notion what God is doing with us. At times it seems as if he has laid upon us more struggle or suffering than we can possibly bear. But the message of our text is, "Hold on! Cleave to God! Believe that he is working his good purpose in you! Refuse to let him go until you receive his blessing!" For Jacob received his blessing, and so will we, good Christians. And that blessing is new life, peace that the world cannot ever give, joy in the companionship of God, meaning and purpose for all of living, and good, highest good, to all eternity.

Lutheran Option: Isaiah 55:1-5

These verses form the first part of the final summons of Second Isaiah (Isaiah 40-55) to the Israelites who are exiles in Babylonia about 550 B.C. These verses and those in 6-7, are surrounded by the promises of a liberating and gracious God, who will deliver his people Israel from their captivity.

What this summons sets forth are the conditions in the state of salvation that Israel will enjoy if she believes the prophet's words and "waits" for God's liberating act (cf. 40:31), and gives her whole heart to her Lord. As such, the words of this text hold out before us, too, the blessings we will have when we commit ourselves, body and soul, to Jesus Christ.

Obviously, the blessings we will receive are described metaphorically. First, the text tells us that we will have the necessities of life — water to drink and bread to eat. When we thirst and hunger, God in his salvation of us will supply our need. If we seek first the Kingdom of God, the Lord knows that we need the necessities of life and will furnish us with them (cf. Matthew 6:25-33).

But the gifts God gives in his salvation of us go far beyond the basic necessities. He will not only give bread and water, but wine and milk and satisfaction in labor (vv. 1-2), enjoyments that stretch far beyond our elemental needs. We will be able to enjoy life, to revel in it, to celebrate, as in a banquet of the choicest delicacies and finest foods.

And even more, says our text, if we commit ourselves to the Lord, we will live (v. 3). And not only that. We will enjoy an everlasting fellowship with our God. The promises to David in the Old Testament (2 Samuel 7:8-16; 23:5; Psalm 89:28-37) are now given to all of God's people — God's steadfast love forever, God's protection from all enemies, God's abiding companionship that even death will not disturb.

As King David's reign was a witness to the power of God, so our salvation will be an equal witness (v. 4), and others also will come to worship the Lord, because they will recognize in our lives that God is with us (v. 5; cf. Zechariah 8:23; Isaiah 2:3). And all of that will serve to glorify the Lord through us.

In many ways, this is a fantastic promise of what commitment to the Lord Christ brings with it. But God always keeps his promises, and countless Christians through the ages can testify to us that yes, their love for Jesus Christ, has brought them salvation's blessings beyond all measure, pressed down and running over. Fullness of life is to be had in the company of our Lord, good Christians. We have only to open our hearts to the gifts he wants to give us.

Proper 14

Genesis 37:1-4, 12-28

Here begins the collection of Joseph stories with which the rest of Genesis will be concerned. There are some contradictions within our text because we have the two sources of the Yahwist and the Elohist woven together. In verses 21-22, it is the northern forbear Reuben, born of Leah, who would save Joseph's life. In verses 26-27, it is Judah from the South. In verse 27, Joseph is to be sold to some passing Ishmaelites, but in verse 28, Midianite traders are the ones passing by. The interweaving of the two sources now serves to involve both northern and southern forbears in the rescue of Joseph from death, as well as to highlight the indecisiveness of the brothers about what to do with their young sibling.

But let's face it. Joseph is a brat, the spoiled youngest son of Jacob's old age, who is his father's favorite and a brash braggart at that. He rashly tells his brothers and parents about his dreams of superiority over them (vv. 5-11). And he lazes about in his long-sleeved coat, while his brothers have to work to tend the flocks. (The correct text says that the coat is not many-colored, but rather it has long sleeves which are for dress and not for work.) It is little wonder that Joseph's eleven brothers hate him and just want to be rid of him. Some of the brothers despise Joseph so much that they want to kill him, but the cooler heads of Reuben and Judah forestall that vengeance. So they settle for selling Joseph as a slave to the Midianite or Ishmaelite traders who are on their way to Egypt. In Egypt, the traders then sell the young lad to Potiphar, the captain of Pharaoh's guard (39:1).

Joseph is obviously an obedient son of his adoring father. When Jacob bids Joseph seek out his shepherding brothers to inquire after their welfare, Joseph immediately obeys (37:13). But he gets lost on the way. When he cannot find his brothers at Shechem, he wanders around in the hill country until a stranger tells him that the brothers have moved their flocks to Dothan, some miles north of Shechem in the region of Samaria. There the brothers are located, but Joseph has made a long trek from Hebron in the south to Dothan in the north.

The brothers, however, have no thought of offering Joseph food and drink and rest from his long journey. Instead, some of them immediately plot Joseph's death, and the words that they speak become a prophecy of everything that follows. "Here comes this dreamer," the brothers say. "Come now, let us kill him ... and we shall see what shall become of his dreams" (vv. 19-20).

Those prophetic words are quoted on a plaque on the motel in Memphis where Martin Luther King, Jr., was staying when he was killed. There could not be a more apt use of this quotation from the Joseph story, for the saying concerns the dreams of a dreamer — Joseph in our text, and Martin Luther King, Jr., in our time. "We shall see what shall become of his dreams."

What the brothers of Joseph did not realize and what our society has not always realized is that the dreams of Joseph and of M. L. King. Jr., were not made up by the human dreamers. No. The dreams came from God. They were the sign and the foretaste of the plan that God was working out in the Genesis story and that he is working out in our world.

God had to send Joseph ahead into Egypt in order to save his people in the time of famine, and God used the dreams of Joseph and the hatred of his brothers to accomplish that plan. And surely, God had to raise up a man with a dream to begin the destruction of the awful race prejudice that lay like a blanket over our land.

As we shall see in Genesis, Joseph's dreams came true, because they were God's dreams. Is it not possible that the dream of Martin Luther King, Jr., will come true also, because it comes from God? Our hatreds and prejudices are no match for the working of God, and we should be very cautious when we think to oppose him.

188

Lutheran Option: 1 Kings 19:9-18

The time in our text is toward the beginning of the reign of the northern king of Israel, Ahab (ca. 869-850 B.C.), the son and successor of the great king, Omri. Ahab is highly successful in military battles, defeating the Syrians to the north and helping to turn back the incursion of the Assyrian Empire. He built magnificent buildings and dominated the southern kingdom of Judah, marrying his daughter Athaliah to Judah's king Jehoram.

Ahab himself is married to Jezebel, a daughter of the king of Tyre, and therein lies his difficulty. Jezebel is a worshiper and promoter of the cult of Baal, the nature god of fertility. As a result, Israel is saturated with idolatry and syncretism. Altars to the Lord are torn down, some of his prophets are put to death, and covenant faithfulness has become a thing of the past.

One man dares to defy Jezebel, however — Elijah the Tishbite. In a contest with 400 of the prophets of Baal on Mount Carmel, Elijah shows them to be false prophets and demonstrates the sole deity of the Lord, who alone rules over all of nature, through famine and deluge (1 Kings 17). Consequently, the 400 prophets of Baal are slain, and in revenge, Jezebel vows to kill Elijah. So in our text, Elijah is fleeing for his life to Horeb (Sinai), "the mount of God," in the Arabian peninsula. It is there on the mount that God encounters his fleeing prophet. (Probably verses 9b-11a are to be omitted from our text as duplicates of verses 11b and 14).

As is often the case with a theophany or appearance of the Lord, there are cosmic disturbances — a great wind, an earthquake, and fire. But the text is careful to distinguish God from natural occurrences (vv. 11-12). God is not "in" any of those phenomena. The Lord of hosts is no nature deity. Instead, God comes to his prophet in his Word — "a voice of thin silence," the most mysterious of descriptions.

When God asks Elijah why he has fled, the prophet tells of the dreadful situation in Israel and claims that he alone is still faithful to the Lord. That is almost a blasphemous statement, for it implies that God has ceased to work among his covenant people in the North. It also has about it a certain self-righteousness, as if

Elijah is saying, "Everyone else is false, and I alone am true," a statement that we sometimes hear from some angry church member in our day, who decides to abandon his church membership and leave behind all of those horrible sinners and hypocrites in the congregation.

Amazingly, God does not rebuke his self-congratulatory prophet. Instead, the Lord tells Elijah to get to work and, indeed, to start a revolution. Elijah is commanded to topple the powerful Omri dynastry represented by Ahab and Jezebel, to replace Ben-Hadad on the throne of Syria with the commoner Hazael, and to anoint Elisha as his prophetic successor (vv. 15-16). That's a tall order, but it demonstrates the power of the God who not only rules all nature but also the kingdoms of the earth. It's as if the Lord is telling his prophet, "You think I'm not at work, Elijah? Think again! I not only preserve the pure faith of 7,000 people in Israel. I also will work through you and through your successor to bring down kings by my mighty Word."

The story is a powerful witness to us. There are many times when it seems to us as if God has lost all control, as if we alone are faithful in the midst of our chaotic society, and as if the rest of humanity is pursuing its rebellious way. But the testimony is: "Remember! Remember the lordship of this mighty God and Father of our Lord Jesus Christ! Remember that he is King of kings and Lord of lords, and is working out his purpose for his world! Remember that death itself could not defeat him, and that his will be the victory over all faithlessness, all evil, all the powers that oppose him!" And then get to work, good Christians! Serve his purpose in your life! And then rejoice that his is the kingdom and the power and the glory forever!

Proper 15

Genesis 45:1-15

In Sunday schools and Bible studies, the Joseph stories are frequently used as moral lessons, and Joseph is often held up as a moral example. As Joseph learned humility, goes the teaching, so should we. As Joseph forgave his brothers, so should we.

It is very doubtful that any character in the Bible, other than our Lord himself, should be pictured as a model of morality, for all have some flaw or commit some sin. In Joseph's case, certainly he develops into an admirable person. But to hold up Joseph as an example is actually to miss the major point of his story. As in all of the scriptures, the major actor and subject of the Joseph stories is God himself, and it is to God's working that our text finally points.

We begin with a moving scene. To test his brothers' characters and familial love, Joseph has hidden a silver cup — a sacred object used for divining — in the baggage of Benjamin, who is departing Egypt with his ten brothers. The penalty for stealing a sacred object is death, but when Joseph accuses the brothers of stealing the cup, he makes them agree that whoever is found with the cup will become Joseph's slave. Of course the cup is found with Benjamin. But Judah pleads with Joseph to let him become Joseph's slave instead of Benjamin, for if their father Jacob loses his youngest surviving child, he will die from grief (ch. 44).

As our text opens, Joseph is overcome with emotion at Judah's sacrificial offer and must finally reveal his identity to his dismayed brothers (vv. 1-3). The speech that Joseph then delivers to his brothers, in verses 4-8, marks the central theological point of these stories in Genesis 37-50. Through all of the vicissitudes of Joseph's life, it is God who has been working to fulfill his promise.

God promised Jacob and his father and grandfather before him that they would have many descendants and a land to call their own. But in this period of the fourteenth century B.C., Canaan and

Egypt are subjected to seven years of drought and famine. The twelve forebears of Israel and their families are threatened with death from starvation. But if that happens, God cannot keep his promise to the patriarchs. Israel must be saved. And so the Lord sends Joseph ahead into Egypt to learn from Pharaoh's dreams of the coming famine and to instruct the Pharaoh to save up food for the whole region during the seven years of plenty preceding the famine. By that method, God sustains his chosen people (and the Egyptians) alive, in order that he may fulfill his Word.

The manner in which God works out this scheme of salvation is simply amazing. First, he uses the hatred of the brothers to prompt them to sell Joseph into slavery in Egypt. Sold into the house of Potiphar, Joseph rises in favor in Potiphar's household. But falsely accused of trying to seduce Potiphar's wife, Joseph is thrown into prison. There, however, he interprets the Pharaoh's dream about the seven fat cows and the seven lean cows, which wins his release from jail and his rise to power as Pharaoh's right hand man. Thus, from that position, Joseph is able to store up the grain that will keep Israel alive. What a convoluted, totally human story it seems, full of suspense and good and evil! But it shows clearly how God is able to use human emotions and activities in order to further his good purpose.

God does not cause human evil, but he uses even it, because his plan for his world moves steadily forward — hidden, unseen, but pressing toward his loving goal. When we think God is absent from our world, therefore; when we believe that all is lost and cruel circumstances have overwhelmed us; then is when we perhaps should most remember the story of Joseph.

Lutheran Option: Isaiah 56:1, 6-8

In 538 B.C., Cyrus of Persia issued a decree that allowed the exiles in the former region of Babylonia to return to their home-land and to rebuild the temple, even furnishing the financial means for the reconstruction (cf. Ezra 1). Some of the exiles returned, under the leadership of the Zadokite priests, but some who had settled down in Babylonia, who had married, built houses, and established businesses (cf. Jeremiah 29:1-7) remained in that foreign country.

Those who returned to Jerusalem faced a very difficult situation. Their city and temple were in ruins, poverty and inflation were rampant, and the agriculture of the peasants who had remained behind in Jerusalem was meager at best. Living was hard-scrabble.

In the midst of that difficult situation, Third Isaiah (Isaiah 56-66) picks up the former message of his predecessor, Second Isaiah (Isaiah 40-55), and announces that God's salvation is near (v. 1). God is returning to his people, to restore their lives. Third Isaiah's call, therefore, is for the people to respond by establishing justice, that is, God's order, in their community, and by doing righteousness, that is, by fulfilling their covenant obligations of love and trust and obedience to their Lord. The prophet calls for such a response, not in order that God might return to them, but because God was in fact returning to be with his chosen people. Obedience and love toward God do not win God's favor, but are responses to the love that God has previously poured out upon us.

Third Isaiah is aware, however, of the plans for the rebuilt community that the Zadokite priestly leaders have already formulated while they are still in Babylonia. The Zadokite priests, and the priestly editors of the Old Testament, were concerned to prevent Israel ever again from falling into sin and deserving the calamity of an exile. The future plans that the priests therefore made for the rebuilt Israelite community were exclusivistic. They wanted all foreign wives excluded from that community (cf. Ezra 9-10). They planned careful attention to ritual and cultic duties. They limited the priesthood to Zadokites, descendants of Aaron. And they banned all foreigners from even worshiping in the rebuilt temple (cf. Ezekiel 44:6-9).

In the Isaianic tradition that is set forth for us in the whole of the Isaiah corpus, however, such exclusivism is not to be found. First and Second Isaiah both announced a universalism that had included foreigners among the saved in Israel (cf. Isaiah 2:2-4; 19:19-25; 42:1-4; 44:5; 45:22-23; 49:6). And indeed, pre-exilic Israel had never excluded the worshiping foreigner from the temple (cf. Exodus 12:48-49; Numbers 15:14-16). From the beginning, Israel's faith looked forward to the blessing of all the families of the earth (Genesis 12:3), and in the figure of the Suffering Servant in Second Isaiah, Israel was called to give its life for the sake of foreign nations (Isaiah 52:13—53:12).

Our text from Third Isaiah therefore continues this universal announcement (vv. 6-8). All faithful people who love the Lord, who keep the sabbath (one of the distinguishing marks of Jewish faithfulness in the exile), and who cling to God in covenant trust will be welcome in the rebuilt temple. They may, in a priesthood of all believers, offer their sacrifices upon the altar, for the temple will be a house of prayer for all peoples (cf. Mark 11:17; Luke 19:46). God is gathering not only his scattered Jewish people to himself, but many others outside of Israel — a fact that came true in the ministry of Jesus and of Paul, who became Christ's apostle to the Gentiles.

Because of the wideness of God's mercy, you and I — we Gentiles — now have become, through faith in Jesus Christ, members of his covenant people begun with Israel. And we are bidden by our Lord to take his good news of eternal salvation to all nations, baptizing them in God's triune name, and teaching them all that Jesus has commanded (Matthew 28:20). There are no barriers to the worship of the God and Father of Jesus Christ, except that of love and trust in him, and faithful response to his saving Word.

Proper 16

Exodus 1:8 — 2:10

With this text, there now occurs a long gap of time in the biblical history of Israel. Jacob and Joseph and his eleven brothers and all their offspring have kept their flocks around the fertile delta of the Nile River in the region of Goshen. But as we read in the priestly introduction of Exodus 1:1-7 to our morning's text, all of that generation finally dies, and at the beginning of our lesson, we read the ominous sentence, "Now there arose a new king over Egypt, who did not know Joseph."

Scholars are reasonably certain that the "new king" was Seti I, who ruled Egypt from ca. 1309-1290 B.C. The facts we are given in verse 11 of our text tell us that the Pharaoh built store-cities at Pithom and Raamses, and those, along with numerous other constructions, were begun in the reign of Seti I. The city of Raamses was called by that name only until the eleventh century B.C., when it was renamed Tanis. And when the Israelites finally escaped from Egypt, they encountered both Edom and Moab in the wilderness (Numbers 20-21), but neither of those kingdoms was established before 1300 B.C. Thus, we are dealing in the book of Exodus with actual history, and our text probably recounts events that took place during the beginning of the reign of Seti.

As is always the case in the biblical story, God has a hand in these historical events, however. The people of Israel multiply rapidly and spread throughout the land of the lower Nile. That is not a notice of Israelite fertility, but of God's working to keep his promise to the patriarchs. God promised Abraham that his descendants would be as many as the stars in the heavens (Genesis 15:5), and that promise is now being fulfilled. That is what our narrator wants to impress upon us.

But of course human fears and follies always arise to try to place obstacles in the way of God's activity. And so Pharaoh Seti,

195

seeing the rapid spread of the Israelites, is afraid that they will join forces with some enemy and overthrow his throne. As a result, he enslaves the Israelites and sets them to hard labor on his many building projects (vv. 9-14). In addition, the royal order is given that all midwives are to kill any Israelite male child that they deliver onto their knees as they sit on the birthstool. Significantly, the names of just two midwives are given, an indication of still how small is the Israelite population (vv. 15-16).

"But the midwives feared God" (v. 17), that is, they are obedient to God and honor his gift of newborn life. The faithful women do not kill the newborns. They make excuses to the Pharaoh, and Israel continues to multiply. Desperate, the Pharaoh finally orders all male children under two years of age to be thrown into the Nile and drowned (v. 22).

The child who is to become Moses is introduced into the story. When his mother sees that she can no longer hide the "goodly child," the healthy child, from Pharaoh's slaughter, she cradles him in a little waterproof basket and hides the basket among the Nile reeds, instructing her daughter Miriam to watch to see what happens. And how fortuitous! — or is it the guiding of God? When the daughter of Pharaoh comes to the site to bathe, she discovers the hidden basket and takes pity on the crying child, deciding to raise him in the royal palace as her son. Miriam, seeing her opportunity, comes out of her hiding place and offers to find a wet nurse for the child — the child's own mother, who not only gets to nurse and raise her infant for at least three years, but is paid for doing so! And finally, in the most ironic touch of all, Pharaoh's daughter names the child "Moses," which comes from the Hebrew *mashah*, "to draw out." Pharaoh's household will become the nurturer of Pharaoh's future opponent, who will "draw out" Israel from slavery!

The passage forms a wondrous account of God's activity in human life, through human fear and faithfulness, human love and pity. Once again, the unseen Lord is at work to keep his promise. But note by what a slender thread God's working hangs. It depends on the obedience of two faithful midwives, on the love of a mother for her newborn, on a flimsy basket that does not leak, on a watching older sister, and on the pity of a royal daughter. At any point in the story, the thread could break and God's purpose could be thwarted. But it does not break and the divine plan moves forward.

Is there not a lesson for us in the tale? A lot of seemingly insignificant events take place in our lives, and we make lots of choices. At the time, how we choose seems to be of no consequence whatsoever. The smallest decision we make, we think, certainly will not affect the outcome of history or the working out of God's purpose for humankind. But could it be that if we are faithful and make decisions and choices that we know are right and according to God's will, those are gathered up and used by Almighty God in his ongoing purpose? In every action, every thought, every decision of our lives, God has a stake. He asks only that we be faithful, in whatever little corner of his world he has placed us, and concerning whatever little task he has given us.

Lutheran Option: Isaiah 51:1-6

How do we know God will keep his Word? Certainly he has made lots of promises to us human beings. To the exiles in Babylonia through the words of Second Isaiah he promised deliverance, a new exodus, a new Eden paradise, a new age of joy that would encompass the earth. And to us he has promised forgiveness of sins, eternal life, and his kingdom come.

Our passage points out one of the ways we can be reassured about God's faithfulness to his Word. "Look to the rock from which you were hewn," God tells captive Israel, "Look to Abraham your father and to Sarah who bore you" (vv. 1-2). "I kept my promises to them," God is saying. "I promised Abraham that he would be the father of a great nation with many descendants, and that has come to pass" (v. 2).

In other words, God kept his promises to Israel — not only the promise of descendants, but of land, of covenant, and of blessing. That is one of the functions of the Old Testament for us Christians — that it tells the story of the centuries through which God kept his Word. Indeed, the Lord finally fulfilled his promises to Israel in

Jesus Christ, summing up all that had gone before in Israel's life, so that Paul can write, "All the promises of God find their 'Yes' in him" (2 Corinthians 1:20). Can we doubt, then, that God will keep his promises to us that he has given through our Lord? Surely the resurrection is the final confirmation of all that God has said!

There is another promise given in our text for the morning. In verse 6, God tells us through his prophet that heaven and earth will pass away, but that his deliverance will never be ended and his salvation will be forever. In an atomic age, surely that is comfort for our anxious hearts. We may blow the earth off its axis, in our human sin and greed and pride, but those who trust God will be taken into an eternal kingdom that will never end. Nothing will separate us from the love of God in Christ Jesus our Lord, good Christians — nothing that human beings can devise or do. And in that love we can have joy and hope and certainty forevermore.

Proper 17

Exodus 3:1-15

Moses, who was raised in the palace of the Pharaoh, has had to flee Egypt, because it has become known that he killed an Egyptian who was beating a Hebrew. He takes flight to Midianite territory in the northwestern section of the Arabian peninsula and takes up residence there with the family of Jethro, a priest of Midian. Content to remain in Jethro's camp, he marries Jethro's daughter, Zipporah, and has a son by her (2:11-22). And he becomes one of the herdsmen of that nomadic tribe, pasturing the flocks near the site of Mount Horeb or Sinai. It is a very ordinary peaceful existence. But Moses' life is not to be ordinary or peaceful. God encounters him through the medium of a bush that is aflame but not consumed. In simple naivete, Moses turns aside to see what has caused such a phenomenon.

Some commentators would like to turn the bush's flame into a normal happening, maintaining that it possesses a natural flame-like foliage, or that it has a resin that sometimes ignites in the heat. But the point of the story is that nothing here is "natural" and earthly. God is on the scene, and God is not encompassed within the sphere of this world. Moses must remove his shoes, because where God is, there is the supernatural realm of holiness, with all its power, and there Moses must not even look, for no man can see the glory of God and live.

God uses the burning bush to get Moses' attention, but it is with his Word that God communicates with the shepherd, just as it is finally by his Word, speaking through scripture and sermon, that God communicates with us. And the central message of God's Word is always that of mercy. God *sees* the affliction of his enslaved people, God *hears* their cry for help from whatever corner, God *knows* their suffering, and God will come down to deliver them (vv. 7-8; cf. 2:24-25). Is that not always the love of God that is poured out upon us — that our Lord sees and hears and knows our lives of enslavement to sin and death; that he hears our prayers for deliverance; and that he comes down in his Son to share our suffering and even our death? The love of God is manifested toward his people from the very beginning here in the Old Testament, and this story foreshadows our lives and our deliverance by our Lord Jesus Christ.

For Israel, the God of love and mercy selects this ordinary shepherd Moses to return to Egypt and to bring his people out of slavery. Moses knows his own capacities and his ordinary station, and not only here, but repeatedly in the accounts that follow, Moses tries to reject the leadership role. The truth is, however, that Moses does not have to rely on himself. "I will be with you," God assures him, "and will lead my delivered people back to this mountain" (v. 12).

Moses, however, has no previous acquaintance with this God who has confronted him, and neither do his enslaved people. The Lord has told him that the One who speaks to him is the same God who spoke to his father and grandfather and great-grandfather before him. His forbears knew this God, but the present generation of Israelites do not. How do they know they can trust his Word? — a question that always arises when we have no acquaintance with God. If Moses can learn the God's name, then he can summon the deity to come to their aid. So Moses asks God's name.

There have been various scholarly translations of what the Lord replies. In Hebrew, he says 'ehyeh 'asher 'ehyeh. Popularly, that has been rendered, "I am who I am." But a lot of linguistic evidence points to the fact that what the name means is "I will indeed be with you," a promise encompassed in "Yahweh," the Hebrew name for the Lord. God has assured Moses that he will be with him, in verse 12. But that hasn't been enough for Moses. He wants a guarantee by learning God's name, in order to be able to command God to his side. The Lord God of hosts is not commanded, however, by any human being. And so, when asked his name, God repeats his promise, "I will indeed be with you." And ever after, Israel is to call God by the name of "He who is indeed with you." With that promise alone, Moses is to return to Egypt and confront the ruler of the Egyptian Empire. Moses' faith is to consist in clinging to God's promise.

Is that not also the one assurance given to us as we struggle through life? Jesus Christ promises us, "Lo, I am with you always, to the end of the age" (Matthew 28:20). We have no other guarantee than that. We are required to walk by faith and not by sight, to cling to that promise and to believe it when all the evidence seems to contradict it. But the Lord who makes that promise to us delivered us from our slavery to sin and death, and made us children of God, and showed us by an empty tomb that he is the victor over all of life's ills and even death. The Lord is with us. He is faithful. And in the power of his Spirit, we can stand, come what may.

Lutheran Option: Jeremiah 15:15-21

We know more about the inner life of the prophet Jeremiah than about any other prophet of the Old Testament, because we have this passage and others like it, called "Jeremiah's Confessions" (cf. 17:14-18; 20:7-12, 14-18). They come from the end of the seventh century B.C., when Jeremiah's prophecies of judgment on Judah have not yet been fulfilled.

Jeremiah has preached and preached that disaster is coming upon his sinful people, as the Lord has given him utterance, and nothing has happened. His words haven't come to pass. As a result, he has become a laughing stock among his compatriots (cf. 20:7) and is daily persecuted by them (15:15). In his situation of distress, he therefore becomes blasphemous toward God, accusing God of being to him a "deceitful brook" (v. 18), of being like one of those wadis in the desert that run with water after the spring rains, but that quickly dry up and yield nothing.

Jeremiah cannot understand what God has done to him. God gave him his words. They certainly came from the Lord, from outside of the prophet and not from his own mind or musings or conscience — such is the meaning of "Thy words were found, and I ate them" (v. 16). And those words were a source of joy to the prophet, because God paid him the honor of being a servant and prophet of his Lord. Despite Jeremiah's initial hatred of the task, he had found satisfaction in being called by God's name and by entering into intimate communion with his Lord.

His role, however, had been a hard one from the first. Jeremiah had to become a "sign," a sign that God was withdrawing his grace from Judah, and so Jeremiah was allowed no manifestations of the grace of God. He couldn't marry; he couldn't attend a party; he could not even go to a funeral, because all of those were gifts of God's grace. So, he says, "I sat alone, because thy hand was upon me" (v. 17). God had deceived him, he thought, and he cries out in our text in anger and anguish.

Usually such laments are followed in the Old Testament by assurances of God's comfort and salvation, but not here. Instead, God rebukes his prophet. Jeremiah had been unfaithful. He had spoken words that were "worthless" and that were not God's words. He needed to repent and return to the Lord (v. 19). If he would do so, God would be with him and enable him to stand against all his persecutors. God would deliver Jeremiah, but Jeremiah had to be faithful (vv. 19-21).

You and I are not prophets of the Lord, but certainly when we are confronted by the struggles and sufferings of life, we, too, cry out, "How could God do this to me?" or "God has deserted me!" But perhaps we need to ask ourselves first of all, "Have I deserted God?" The Lord promises always to be with us, but we know joy and comfort and assurance from that fact only when we have not forgotten his presence, but have turned in every circumstance faithfully to him.

Proper 18

Exodus 12:1-14

This particular text, which tells of the institution of the Jewish Passover feast, is to mark the beginning of the year in the month of Abib (March-April) for the Hebrews (v. 2). Originally, the New Year began in the fall with the harvest (cf. 23:16; 34:22), but it was switched to the spring by the priestly writers of the sixth century B.C., who followed the Babylonian calendar.

It may seem strange that this text is now assigned to us for September. We usually associate Passover with Maundy Thursday before Easter, when our Lord eats his final Passover meal with his disciples before he goes out to be crucified. But are we not too at the beginning of a new season in our church schedule? Everyone has returned from vacation. The children will shortly be back in school. Church school classes and choir practices are resuming, and we are entering our fall schedule of worship services. So, like the Israelites in our text, we are at a beginning, and this text has a good deal to say to us about how to conduct ourselves.

First of all, this text has to do with travelers who are on the move. The Israelites are about to be delivered by the Lord out of their old life of captivity in Egypt. And so everything they do in this Passover festival is to be characteristic of travelers who are on the verge of leaving. For their food, they are to select a lamb of a sheep or goat and to roast it over an open fire, where no utensil or boiling water is needed. They are to eat unleavened bread, because there is not time for their bread to rise, and their spices are to be bitter herbs that are pulled straight from the ground. Their loins are to be girded, that is, their long robes are to be gathered up about their hips and tied there with a belt, so they can walk freely. Their feet are to be shod for walking, and they are to have their hiking staffs in hand, ready for departure. They are to be prepared to journey.

So too, good Christians, as we start this fall in our church year, we are to be prepared for moving on, because the Christian life is never a static acceptance of the status quo. It is pressing forward toward God's goal for us. God never lets us remain just as we are. He wants us to know more about the Bible's contents and about his words revealed through those contents, and so we are to press on in our Bible study and in our daily private Bible reading, enlarging our knowledge of our Lord. God in his love desires that we deepen our communion and daily fellowship with him, and so he asks us to commit ourselves to more regular private prayer and to more heartfelt and sincere corporate worship, that we may grow in sanctification and goodness. God sees all of his beloved people out there in our neighborhoods and world who desperately need to hear of his forgiveness and new life, and so he asks us to increase our efforts in evangelism and mission, drawing more members into this church and increasing our activities on the mission field. And God knows that everywhere there are people who are suffering, in hunger or poverty, sickness or anxiety, and he asks us to rekindle our efforts to love our neighbors and to minister to their needs. We are at a beginning once again in this September, but there's no resting on our laurels, no doing things as we have always done them. God says to us, "Be prepared to journey, move on, press forward in the discipleship which I have given you!"

Why? Because, like the Israelites prepared to depart Egypt, good Christians, God is going to "pass over" us and deliver us from our slavery. No. He's not *going* to do it. He already has, in the cross and resurrection of his Son. Through the work of Jesus Christ, you and I have been delivered from our slavery also, our slavery to sin and death. God has given us a foretaste of "the glorious liberty of the children of God," as he gave it to Israel, and he has set us free to live a new life, as Israel was set free. And we, like that first people of God, are on the journey to a promised land — a promised land called not Palestine this time, but called the Kingdom of God. So let's move on, beloved Christians! Forgetting what lies behind, let us press on toward the upward call of God in Christ Jesus, until his kingdom does indeed come on earth, even as it is in heaven!

Lutheran Option: Ezekiel 33:7-11

This passage from Ezekiel details for us one of the functions of a prophet in Israel, namely to be a "watchman." A loosely parallel passage is found in Ezekiel 3:16-21, and the similar watchman function of a prophet is mentioned in Hosea 9:8; Jeremiah 6:17; and Isaiah 56:10. Like a watchman set on the wall of a city to warn it of the approach of an enemy, the prophets were to warn the Israelites of God's approaching judgment on their sin. Ezekiel understands God to be the "enemy" of sin (cf. 13:1-5), as do all of the pre-exilic prophets. And God the enemy can destroy Israel for her sin against him.

This particular passage deals primarily with the sin of individuals. If the prophet warns some sinner of God's approaching judgment, but the sinner does not repent and amend his life, the sinner will die for his iniquity. But if the prophet does not warn a sinner and the sinner dies, the fault will be also the prophet's and the prophet too will die. In short, the prophet is held responsible for the life of his compatriots! He *must* pass on God's word to sinners or forfeit his own life.

Two emphases speak to us out of this text. First is the life and death importance of the Word of God. God's word as it is given to us in the gospel is not a mere suggestion or an instruction that can be accepted or rejected as we will. No. God's word involves life or death. As we learn also from the New Testament, it involves whether any person will have eternal life or death. And so it is absolutely important for everyone we meet and everyone in the world that we pass on the good news of the gospel to them.

Preachers are sometimes asked, "What will happen to all of those people in the world who have never heard the gospel when the last judgment takes place?" The reply can only be that they are in the hands of the merciful God whom we have known in Jesus Christ.

But this text adds a second thought to that reply. It tells us that if we have the opportunity to tell a sinful world and sinful individuals about the forgiveness and salvation possible to them in

Christ, and they die because we have not told them, *we are responsible for their death!* We have not passed on the good news to them that could give them eternal life, and so we too stand under the judgment of God.

In other words, part of our function and responsibility in the Christian faith is to pass it on. In our mission work, at our jobs, in our social circles, and especially in our families and to our children, we are to communicate God's word. We can do it by what we speak, by how we act toward others, and by the way we conduct our daily lives. Our words, our actions, our standards, and ethics — all are to show forth our faith. And if we do not do that, as God's servants and disciples, God holds us responsible.

That seems like a fearful calling. But the comforting part is that God not only commands us to pass on the Christian faith. He also pours into our hearts his Holy Spirit, giving us the strength, the guidance, the wisdom, to be his witnesses in our daily lives and in our world. We too are "watchmen and watchwomen" for the Lord, good Christians. And we are called to be faithful at our posts.

Proper 19

Exodus 14:19-31

The exodus from slavery in Egypt and the deliverance of the Israelites from the pursuing troops of Pharaoh Raamses II at the Sea of Reeds ca. 1280 B.C. forms the central redemptive act in the Old Testament. That redemption is mentioned in almost every book of the Old Covenant and still today it is commemorated by Jews all over the world at their Passover feasts.

There is no doubt that the exodus happened, and there is no reputable scholar who seriously questions the event. But because the story of the deliverance at the sea has accrued layers of tradition, we cannot say exactly what happened. In our text, three sources are woven together to describe the event, with some disagreements among them. In the Yahwist source, the Lord drives back the sea with a strong east wind. According to the priestly writers, the sea is divided when Moses stretches forth his hand. In the brief excerpts from the Elohist sources, there are echoes of the Holy War tradition, in which the Lord discomfits the Egyptians and clogs their chariot wheels.

All of the sources and, indeed, the Old Testament as a whole, agree however that the event was solely the work of God and that Israel was the passive recipient of his act of love (cf. vv. 13-14). Israel did nothing to effect her redemption; the Lord did it all.

The New Testament parallel to this text is the story of the cross. As Israel was delivered from slavery at the Sea of Reeds, so we were delivered from our slavery to sin and death by the cross and resurrection of Jesus Christ. In fact, when Jesus talks about his coming crucifixion in Luke 9:31, he terms it his "exodus" (translated in the English as "departure"). It is therefore possible for us to understand more fully the crucifixion of our Lord by delving into the meaning of this deliverance of Israel.

First, it is clear that Israel had done nothing to deserve her redemption (her "buying back") from slavery. She had not yet entered into covenant with her Lord; she had not yet received the commandments. She had worked no piety or obedience. And so too we, when we are redeemed by the cross and resurrection of Christ, have done nothing to deserve it. "While we were yet sinners, Christ died for us" (Romans 5:8).

Second, therefore, Israel understood her redemption to be solely an act of God's love (cf. Deuteronomy 7:7-8). He had seen the affliction of slaves whom he claimed as his people, and he came down in love to deliver them (cf. Exodus 2:24-25; 3:7-8). So too is our redemption by God's act in Christ his gift of pure, loving grace toward us. ("God shows his love for us in that while we were yet sinners Christ died for us.")

Third, the redemption of Israel forms an integral part of God's work toward his goal of bringing blessing on all the families of the earth through the descendants of Abraham (cf. Genesis 12:3). It is not an isolated event, but the crucial act of deliverance of a people whom God is using to fulfill his promise. And so too is our redemption a part of God's movement toward the goal of his kingdom come on earth.

Fourth, it was the exodus deliverance that first made Israel a people. They were a "mixed multitude" (Exodus 12:38) when they came out of Egypt, from many different tribes and backgrounds, and it was their redemption in common that bound them together as a people of the Lord. They had all been redeemed together! That was what they all shared and what made them a unity, and if they forgot their redemption, they became "no people" (cf. Hosea 1:8-9, 15). In similar fashion, we in the church are a mixed multitude, from various nations and races, backgrounds and situations. But the one fact that holds us together as one people of God is that we have all been redeemed together by the cross of Christ. If we forget that redemption that we share, our unity becomes impossible and we become "no people" of God, no church.

Fifth, God's destruction of the troops of Pharaoh at the Sea of Reeds is clear evidence of God's dealing with sin. As Martin Luther King, Jr., wrote of our text, "Egypt symbolized evil in the form of

208

humiliating oppression, ungodly exploitation, and crushing domination" (*Strength to Love*, Philadelphia: Fortress Press, 1981, p. 73), and God drowned its power. The wages of its sin was death. And so too, the wages of our sin is death, experienced first on our behalf by our Lord on his cross, and still today for those who would think to defy the Lord of all empire, history, and nature.

God in his love redeemed his people. And that is also our story. For in his love in Jesus Christ, God has also redeemed us.

Lutheran Option: Genesis 50:15-21

At this end of the stories of Joseph, we find his brothers still burdened by their guilt. They are afraid that Joseph will take his vengeance on them and perhaps have them imprisoned or executed. And so they tell one more lie, saying that their father Jacob, before he died, had commanded that the brothers be forgiven their evil actions toward Joseph. Thus do those who commit sin try to save their own skins, through lies, deviousness, self-justifications. "What a tangled web we weave when first we practice to deceive."

But Joseph's acts are not determined by purely human emotions and schemes. Joseph has a clearer vision of what ultimately matters in this world. Joseph has a vision and understanding of the purposes and plans of God. He knows that the Lord is working out his purpose, in fulfillment of his promise to Abraham (Genesis 12:3), to bring his blessing through Israel on all the families of the earth. And Joseph knows that everything that the brothers have done to him and everything that has happened to him in Egypt have been part of that plan of God's, so that God could keep alive his chosen people during the seven years of famine. Joseph therefore can tell his brothers that though they have done evil toward him, God has used that evil for good. Joseph subordinates all of his own feelings and possible desires for vengeance to God, who is doing and always does only good.

Is it not possible, good Christians, that when we surrender our human desires and hatreds, our turbulent emotions and feelings to the Lord, that God always brings out of our sinful ways his good?

We are never perfect Christians, but God is a perfect God. And if we surrender our lives to him, he uses them in his eternal purpose of bringing blessing on this earth.

Certainly the cross of Christ is the supreme example of that. From a purely human standpoint, the cross was terrible — a torturous exhibition of our human sin putting an innocent man to death. But because Christ surrendered himself to the will of his Father and let all our sins nail him to that tree, the Father used that evil to work his highest good — our forgiveness and redemption and the Father's eternal love for all the world shown forth.

Proper 20

Exodus 16:2-15

"Give us this day our daily bread." This text from Exodus forms the background of that petition in the Lord's Prayer. The Israelites have been delivered from slavery in Egypt and are trekking through the wilderness, with all of its dangers, toward the promised land. When they cry out for bread and meat, God sends quails and manna for their food. But only one day's provision of manna is given at a time, except on the sixth day, when there is a double supply to last through the sabbath, a day of rest. Not too much is given for each day and not too little. And if the Israelites try to store up the manna during five days of the week instead of gathering it every day, it rots.

The text tells us that 45 days have passed since the deliverance at the Reed Sea. The people have been encamped at the oasis of Elim, with its copious water and palm trees (15:27), but now they must travel on through the Wilderness of Sin on the way to Mount Sinai. The exact location of both Elim and Sinai cannot be specified, but the Exodus emphasizes that the people move on from place to place "according to the commandment of the Lord" (17:1). They are following an itinerary given them by God.

God is the furthest thought from their minds, however. They are not starving to death, but like so many who prefer comfort to freedom, they long for the "fleshpots" and "bread aplenty" of Egypt (v. 3) — undoubtedly a selective memory (cf. Numbers 11:4-5), especially since meat was a rare delicacy in the Ancient New East. They therefore accuse Moses of wishing to kill them with hunger. They have no real need, but they are greedy. And above all, they have forgotten completely that they are on God's journey, as you and I forget that. The Israelites are testing Moses' leadership and ultimately, God's. But the Israelites — and we — are the ones who are really being tested. Do they and we trust God?

Amazingly, God does not respond to his people's greed and forgetfulness of him with anger. How gracious the Lord always is!

Instead, God sends his people both meat and the bread of manna for their daily fare. While the quail meat is mentioned only in verse 13, the story concentrates on the gift of the manna.

"What is it?" the people wonder (v. 15), and from that question comes its name. "Manna" is *man hu* in the Hebrew, something the people have never seen before. A number of commentators wish to equate manna with a natural substance, emphasizing that God's grace is given even through ordinary things (Terence Fretheim). "The tamarisk bush," writes Kyle McCarter (*Harper's Bible Commentary*, p. 147), "which grows in part of the Sinai Peninsula, is infested with scale insects that suck its sap, some of which is excreted in the form of globules that crystallize in the sun ... This sticky substance is rich in carbohydrates and sugars and can support the life of a starving wanderer. It is still called *mann* by the modern inhabitants of the Sinai, who regard it as a gift from God."

If we let the scriptures interpret the scriptures, however, it is clear that manna is not a natural substance. It is described as white, like coriander seed, and as a wafer with a taste of honey (v. 31). It miraculously supplies just enough for each day and doubles in quantity on the sixth day, and it is stored without rotting in the future temple, along with the tablets of the law, through centuries (vv. 32-34). Psalm 78:24-25 calls it "the grain of heaven" and "the bread of angels." Paul terms it "supernatural food" (1 Corinthians 10:3), and Jesus compares himself to it as the bread of life come down from heaven (John 6: 48-49). In short, the manna with which God feeds the Israelites during their forty years in the wilderness (Exodus 16:35) is a supernatural gift of grace.

The manna is given for two reasons, according to our text. First, it is used as a test of the Israelite's trust in God (v. 4). Will they follow God's command and gather only one day's supply of the manna during the week, or will they ignore God's word and try to hoard the food? Do they trust God to supply their lives every day? Do we? Do we trust that he will fulfill our needs, or are we anxious about the morrow, wondering what we shall eat and what we shall put on (Matthew 6:25)? Are our physical necessities what we concentrate on? Certainly it would seem so from the evidence in our materialistic world.

Second, the manna is given, according to our text, in order that the Israelites may know that "I am the Lord your God" (v. 12). The manna is graciously given by God, though the Israelites do not deserve it, to remind them that they are on God's journey as God's people. They have become "the congregation of the people of Israel" (v. 1) — an unusual phrase in Exodus. They are no longer like every other group of wandering nomads, eating the produce of the desert. Now they are God's special people, dependent always on the Lord their God and sustained in their new life of freedom by his free grace (cf. Deuteronomy 8:3). And so are we. You and I are special people now, good Christians. We are no longer like every other soul, wandering through this wilderness of our world. Now we are God's people, journeying according to his command, toward the promised goal of his kingdom. And at every step along the way, God supplies us through his Holy Spirit with his sustenance and strength, his guidance and free mercy.

That's what the petition, "Give us this day our daily bread," finally means in our Lord's Prayer — not only our material bread, but also our spiritual food. We can't store it up; we are dependent on it every hour and every day. But God gives it to us in his love. And especially does he supply us with that spiritual food when we celebrate together the Lord's Supper. There we feast on the true bread of life come down from heaven in our Lord Jesus Christ, who is able not only to sustain our bodies and minds and spirits now, but who pours out his power upon us to give us eternal life. We have only to make two responses, dear congregation of God — to receive and to trust!

Lutheran Option: Jonah 3:10 — 4:11

The humorous little book of Jonah is really not about a big fish (never called a whale) or about a disobedient prophet (Jonah is never called a prophet). Instead, it is about the free mercy and love of God.

Jonah initially disobeys God's command to go to Nineveh and to preach repentance, because he does not think Nineveh, the capital of the evil Assyrian Empire, should be forgiven.

Certainly that empire was hated throughout the ancient Near East of the eighth century B.C., because it had the cruel policy of destroying tiny nations, of deporting their populations, and of replacing them with foreigners. That is what Assyria did to the ten northern tribes of Israel in 721 B.C. Those ten tribes disappeared from history and were replaced by the hated Samaritans in the northern portion of Israel.

After Jonah is rescued from drowning, however, he does go to Nineveh and preach. And miraculously, that evil nation repents, even down to the last beast in the field. The repentance does not automatically bring God's forgiveness (v. 9), but God does grant it nevertheless in his free mercy (v. 10). And that infuriates Jonah, because for him, that means that there is no structure of justice in the world. To Jonah's way of thinking, the evil should be punished and the good rewarded. But if that doesn't happen, Jonah just wants to die (4:3); life is not worth living if there is no strict justice — and Jonah angrily tells God so (4:1-3). In fact, Jonah sits down east of Nineveh and watches to see if perhaps God will follow his advice after all (4:5).

Amazingly, the God who is rich in mercy, does not chastise his angry prophet. Instead, God just lets Jonah experience a little grace, in the form of a plant shading his head, and a little judgment, in the forms of a worm that eats the plant, and in the form of discomfort caused by the hot sirocco out of the desert (vv. 6-8). And then, God points out to his angry prophet that Jonah's discomfort and faintness were only a hint of judgment and not at all comparable to the judgment that Jonah wanted for Nineveh. Could Jonah, then, not find a little mercy in his heart at least for the children and beasts in Nineveh, and could he not wish for them a little of the grace that God had shown to him? After all, Jonah had been delivered from death and shielded simply out of God's mercy. Could Jonah not wish that also for his fellow human beings?

Those are the questions that we are left with in this little story of Jonah. Given the free grace that God has daily poured out on us sinners like Jonah, who incidentally never does repent, can't we find in our hearts a little wish for mercy toward our fellow sinners — for all those folk whom we judge to be evil and for whom we just wish God's judgment? Can't we?

214

Proper 21

Exodus 17:1-7

The traditions that we find in the Old Testament concerning Israel's wandering in the wilderness after her exodus from Egypt have a recurring pattern that probably dates back to the time when they were told orally (cf. Exodus 15:22-25; Numbers 11:1-3; 20:1-13). It is much easier to remember something if it follows a particular pattern, and the oral pattern of these particular texts shows that they are very old.

In the pattern, Israel confronts a desperate need in the desert — in our text, the need for water. The people murmur against Moses, and he cries out to God. "What shall I do with this people? They are ready to stone me!" (v. 4). In reply, God supplies the need, giving them, in this story, the water that they require. The story is loosely paralleled in Numbers 20:1-13.

But this is a very human bunch that Moses is leading through the wilderness, isn't it? When they get into difficulty, they blame their leaders. And most of the time they forget all about the fact that God has delivered them and is going before them every step of the way, planning their itinerary, even showing them where to make camp (cf. Numbers 10:33-34), feeding them with manna, preventing their clothes and sandals from wearing out (Deuteronomy 29:5), and defending them from their enemies (Exodus 17:8-13). How blind they — and we — often are to the leading and gifts of God! Had the Israelites trusted the Lord and been aware of his constant presence, they themselves could have prayed for water. But no. They have to blame someone else, and poor Moses is in danger of being stoned. It is no wonder that Moses often wishes that God had never saddled him with the leadership of such a people.

God, however, shows his almost inexhaustible patience in these wilderness stories. Constantly he puts up with the people's lack of trust, with their complaints, and with their blindness to his grace.

215

The people constantly put the Lord to the test, and the Lord never fails them, despite their mistrust.

So the Israelites and their cattle are given water to drink from a rock. The fact that the rock is said to be at Horeb, another name for Mount Sinai, is strange in the story, because Israel does not arrive at Sinai until chapter 19. The other traditions mentioning this story locate it at Meribah alone (Numbers 20:13; Psalm 81:7; 106:32). But however that may be, God gives water out of a spring from a rock to a thirsty people, thus preserving them alive in their time of crisis.

That water, like the supernatural food of the manna, was a "supernatural drink," wrote Paul to the Corinthians (1 Corinthians 10:4) — not a natural spring, but a gift of God's mercy. And that rock, continues Paul, was Christ.

In our deepest need, when we thirst — for something — or when we are confronted by the valley of death; when we have no one else to blame and no human helper; when our lack of trust and faithfulness has brought us to the edge of an abyss, and there is no exit and no hope and no future, who is it that can furnish us with the water of life, and with a new beginning? Christ. Christ our Rock. Christ who brings forth the water of eternal life, welling up and overflowing. And by his mercy, our thirst is quenched, good Christians, our valley of death is turned into a place of life, and we are given a new vitality, a new beginning and a new future. Out there ahead of us, as we wander through our wildernesses, there is a place of rest and promise called the Kingdom of God. So, refreshed and renewed by the flowing Spirit of Christ our Rock, let us journey in gladness toward it.

Lutheran Option: Ezekiel 18:1-4, 25-32

Karl Menninger of the famous Menninger Clinic wrote a book way back in 1973 titled *Whatever Became of Sin?* It was one of the most perceptive volumes ever written and went through multiple printings. In that book, Menninger maintained that the principal characteristic of our society is the loss of a sense of responsibility. And that is true, isn't it? For it seems as if very few people any more will take responsibility for what they do.

If someone commits a crime, we don't label them a sinner; we say they must be mentally ill, or under the influence of drugs or alcohol, and so they're not responsible. If we ourselves commit some wrong, we blame it on someone else. "My parents didn't raise me right." Or "I grew up in an evil environment." Or "I've got this psychological hang-up." Or "I goofed. Sorry about that." We don't want to take responsibility for our actions, and especially we do not want to take responsibility to God. "Sin" is an outdated concept, many think, and God does not hold anyone responsible.

Our text for the morning gives the lie to such views, for it tells us plainly that the Lord holds us accountable for all of our deeds. And God does not countenance evil. "The soul that sins shall die" (v. 4). "The wages of sin is death" (Roman 6:23). "We must all appear before the judgment seat of Christ, so that each one may receive good or evil, according to what he (or she) has done in the body" (2 Corinthians 5:10).

If we do evil and repent of our sin and turn away to a new way of acting, however, our text says that God will forgive us and we will not die. Conversely, if we have been doing good, but then turn to evil ways and do not repent, we shall be judged and die for our evil.

Our text and, indeed, the scriptures as a whole also know the seat of our evil. It is in our hearts. As Jesus taught, "From within, out of the heart of a man (or woman) come evil thoughts ... and they defile" us (Mark 7:20, 23). There is the location of our sin — in our hearts — where we store up selfishness and hatreds, grudges and anxieties, fears and greeds. And those come forth from our hearts and corrupt our actions.

Therefore, says our text from Ezekiel, "Get yourselves a new heart and a new spirit. Why will you die, O house of Israel?" We need to be made clean and new in our inner selves, that our outer actions may be good and not bad. We need to be changed from the inside out.

But how can that happen, good Christians? How can all of the selfishness and pride and wickedness that we so often harbor in our hearts be done away and we be made new and good? It's a cinch that we can't cleanse our hearts on our own, can we? We will what is right, but we cannot do it. We do not the good that we want, but instead we do what is wrong (Romans 7:18-19).

But the Lord God sees our plight and our inability to make ourselves new. And so what does he do? He forgives us by the cross and resurrection of his Son, and then he baptizes us into that Son, and raises us to newness of life, and pours into our hearts the Spirit of Christ, giving us the ability to be good and to do what is right. And he says to us, "Come unto me," and all we have to do is to accept that by faith and to let Christ thus rule in our hearts.

Well, the invitation is there, friends. Trust Christ to make you a new person. Come unto him. And God wants so much for us to accept that. For as our text in Ezekiel says, the Lord has no pleasure in the death of anyone. He wants us to live. He wants us to live abundantly and eternally. And if we will — if we will — we can have that abundant and eternal life.

Proper 22

Exodus 20:1-4, 7-9, 12-20

Our story of Israel has brought us to Mount Sinai, where Israel has heard that she is God's elected people, his kingdom of priests and his holy nation, set apart for God's purpose. Upon hearing of her election, she has promised, "All that the Lord has spoken, we will do" (Exodus 19:8). Now she learns what that promise entails. She is given God's commandments in this famous passage of the Decalogue (cf. the parallel in Deuteronomy 5:6-21), and these ten commandments form the absolutely necessary requirements for the life of the people of God. As a result, Jesus quotes some of the commandments (Mark 10:19 and parallels), and lays all of them upon us Christians also, so that the Decalogue forms a summary of how we are to conduct our lives in responsibility to God.

It is exceedingly important that we include verse 2 of our text. Apart from it, the place of law in the scriptures cannot be understood. In that verse, the Lord reminds Israel of what they have seen and experienced: he has delivered them out of their slavery in the land of Egypt. In short, God's merciful act of grace has taken place first before any commandment is given. Obedience to God's commandments therefore is to form Israel's grateful response to what God has already done.

In the same manner we Christians have been delivered from our slavery to sin and death by the cross and resurrection of Christ. Our obedience to Christ's commandments therefore rises out of our gratitude for what God has already done for us. God's grace is always prevenient. God's merciful act always takes place first. And Christian living is then a grateful and answering reply to God's love. "We love because he first loved us."

But, someone may ask: "Why should we be required to obey any commandments at all? Are we not justified and made acceptable to God by faith alone? We cannot work our way into God's favor. That acceptance is given as a free gift to those who believe. So why are we given commandments to obey?"

The answer is twofold, and again it concerns God's grace. We are indeed justified and assured of our salvation through the work of Jesus Christ. We now have a new status and a new life in relation to our God. But how are we to act in this new life which God has given us? How are we to act toward others, and how are we to act toward the Lord? Thanks be, God does not let us wander around in the dark, making up the answers as we go along. Instead, in his love, he continues to guide us. He points the way. ("To point the finger" is the basic meaning of "torah" in the Bible.) He says, "This is the way; walk in it. This is the way you can have abundant life. This is the way to joy and love and peace that passes understanding. This is how it will go well with you" (cf. Deuteronomy 5:29). God wants it always to go well with us, and so, in his love, he guides us by the paths that will lead to our highest welfare. For example, God knows that no marriage in which adultery occurs can be happy or good. And so he says, "You shall not commit adultery" (v. 14). That is a gift of his love and concern for us. And all of the commandments are given out of that concern.

How can we have abundant life? We can rest one day of the week, instead of working ourselves to a frazzle. How can we get along with our parents? We can honor them and respect them. How can we have goodness in our community? By being honest and not stealing and not testifying falsely in court against our neighbors. How can we preserve peace among all humankind? By not killing and not coveting others territory or power or goods. How can we thank and serve God truly? By worshiping only him and by not making idols of anything or anyone else in all creation; by not trying to make him less than he is in accommodation to our thoughts and ways. God wants it to go well with us.

Another fact enters in. As with Israel, God also wants to use us Christians as his holy people, as his instruments to spread the good news of his love and to bring blessing on all the families of the earth. God has loved us because he loves all people, and he wants us to be his witnesses who tell others of that love. So God gives us instructions that will form us into a people who manifest his love.

Then all of those around us can see and know what it means to be God's people. And they can be drawn into that community that lives by the life-giving love of God.

God has poured out his grace on us by redeeming us and by giving us his commandments. We respond in obedient gratitude to his mercy.

Lutheran Option: Isaiah 5:1-7

God's prophet Isaiah, of the eighth century B.C., plays the part of a troubadour in this song of the vineyard. Like troubadours everywhere, he sings a love song, thereby drawing the attention of his listeners in Jerusalem. His song concerns a friend who planted a vineyard with great care, clearing it of stones, planting in it the choicest of grape vines, and setting a watchtower in its midst to ward off ravaging animals and thieves. The friend even hewed out a wine vat in a stone, expecting a yield of the choicest grapes (*'anavim*). But he was deeply disappointed. The vineyard yielded only rotten, stinking wild grapes (*b'ushim*).

Was there anything else the friend could have done? Isaiah's listeners are required to answer the question. And surely, they all agree — "nothing." So the only solution is to pull up the vines and to let the weeds and thorns take over. The vineyard has proven useless. It deserves only to be destroyed. The listeners all concur. But suddenly they are drawn up short by the troubadour, whose song tells them that the friend will not even let rain fall on the vineyard. Rain? What human being can command the clouds and rain? Obviously, none. And so Isaiah can drive home his point from the Word of God.

The vintner is God, and the vineyard is Israel, his "pleasant planting." God showed every care for Israel, bringing them to a land flowing with milk and honey, guiding their life with his commandments and prophets, defending them from their enemies, pouring out his love and forgiveness repeatedly upon them. And God expected that in gratitude, Israel would respond to his love by forming a society of justice (*mishpat*) and righteousness (*tsedekah*).

Instead, Israel's society is shot through with injustice and blood-shed (*mispach*), with cries of violence and alarm (*ts'akah*). All of God's loving care for Israel has been in vain, and God's only recourse is to do away with her rottenness by subjecting her to destruction by the armies of the Assyrian Empire.

That immediately raises burning questions for us, doesn't it? For we too are God's vineyard (Mark 12:1-12 and parallels). "I am the vine, you are the branches," Jesus tells us. And he warns us that every branch of his that bears no fruit is taken away (John 15:5, 2). In other words, God's patience with us can be at an end. God is not mocked, as Paul tells us, "for whatever a man (or woman) sows, that he (or she) will also reap" (Galatians 6:7). We cannot impose on the forgiveness and mercy of God forever. He can destroy us. And we risk our eternal lives when we believe that God only forgives and forgives and overlooks our disobedience and indifference toward him.

To be sure, God has no pleasure in the death of anyone (Ezekiel 18:32). He wants us to live eternally. And he has provided the way to life through his son Jesus Christ. But perhaps this word from the prophet Isaiah tells us, before it is too late, that our repentance and turning are overdue.

Proper 23

Exodus 32:1-14

Our text, which is from the Yahwist, connects with Exodus 24:18, where we are told that Moses is on Mount Sinai with God for forty days and forty nights. The intervening material in chapters 25-31 is from the priestly writers and concerns God's command to make a tabernacle and ark of the covenant. The preacher may want to resume the story with 24:28, followed immediately by 32:1.

This story of the golden calf is so full of sermon material that the preacher has a wide choice of themes for the proclamation. Let us briefly detail them.

First there is the theme of our propensity to sin. As George Buttrick once remarked, "Before we leave the church door, we fall once again into sin." Certainly Israel in this story is an example of that. Here is a people who have been redeemed from slavery and who have just entered into covenant with God, promising, "All that the Lord has spoken, we shall do." But like us, they are an impatient people who want to take matters into their own hands and run their own affairs. Moses hasn't come down from the mountain for forty days and nights. All they are left with as a leader is the priest Aaron, who is quite willing to accede to the rebellious people's wishes. After all, the polls show what the people want! So they tell Aaron, "Make us gods, who shall go before us." Everyone needs some sort of god, and if the true God isn't satisfactory, we'll make our own. And Aaron agrees to that popular position. How quick we are to forget what God has done for us and the long path on which he has led us, and to turn to deities more suited to our preferences!

But second, we should note that the nature of God is defined by what he has done. From the time of the exodus onward, the God of the Old Testament is identified as "the Lord your God, who brought you up out of the land of Egypt," just as God in the New Testament is defined as "the God and Father of our Lord Jesus Christ." Only the deity who has those identifying marks is true God. When Aaron makes the golden calf, therefore, he has to tell the Israelites that the little golden bull he has carved is the one who brought them up out of the land of Egypt. Any rational person knows that is a lie, of course, but the Israelites are easily deceived, because they want it that way. It should be a reminder to us, however, when we start manufacturing our own gods and goddesses that we should ask what deeds they have done. Is the God we worship the deity who freed Israel? Is he the one who sent his only Son to die on a cross and who raised him up on the third day? What has your God done? Has he actually conquered death? Or are his actions on your behalf a figment of your imagination? Has your god done anything at all? Or is he just some amorphous something in the great somewhere? We must be careful to know the characteristics that define who the one true God really is.

Third, we see from this text the intercessory function of the prophets in the Old Testament. Moses is the first and greatest prophet (cf. Numbers 12:6-8), and he begins the function of interceding for his sinful people, pleading with God to turn aside his judgment on Israel's sin (cf. Deuteronomy 9:13-20, 25-29; Amos 7:1-6). Moses makes two appeals to God. He points out that the Lord will be dishonored in the eyes of the Egyptians if he slays his people. But he also reminds God of his promise of land and many descendants to the patriarchs. If God destroys the people in the wilderness, he cannot keep his promise. And that is unthinkable to God. So, says our text, "the Lord repented of the evil which he thought to do to his people" (v. 14). In other words, because of the intercessory prayer of his servant Moses, the Lord God Almighty changed his mind!

We sometimes have the mistaken notion that all of the future is preordained by God, and that therefore intercessory prayer is futile. Not so in the Bible! What we find there is a constant dialogue between God and human beings, in which the Lord takes very seriously the actions and faith and prayers of us mortals. What we do and what we believe and for what we pray make a difference. And so Jesus tells us in the New Testament, "Ask, and it will be given you; seek, and you will find; knock, and it will be opened to you" (Matthew 7:7). And Ephesians tells us, "Pray at all times in the Spirit, with prayer and supplication" (Ephesians 6:18). God hears the prayers of his faithful, and we are to pray for one another, just as Moses and the prophets of old prayed for their sinful folk, trusting that God will answer the prayer in accordance with his love.

Lutheran Option: Isaiah 25:1-9

The lectionary is shaped more by tradition and the content of passages than by form criticism. As a result, it often joins separate forms or breaks apart passages that belong together. That is true of this stated text. What we find here is, first, a song of praise (vv. 1-5), that interrupts the connection between 24:23 and 25:6. Then the proclamation contained in 25:6-9 should be ended before the last sentence of verse 9 ("let us be glad and rejoice in our salvation"). That sentence belongs with verse 10 as the beginning word "For" in verse 10 shows. Nevertheless, we can follow the thought of the passage.

This reading is a part of what is known as the Isaiah Apocalypse that is made up of Isaiah 24-27. Consequently that which is pictured here is the end of history, when God has won his final victory over his enemies and brought in his kingdom, in which he will be worshiped by all nations.

The song of praise in verses 1-5 praises God for his triumph over a ruthless enemy of both Israel and God. God has planned such a triumph from of old, because his plan and goal have always been to establish his kingdom on earth — a fact known most familiarly to us from the Lord's Prayer ("thy kingdom come"). The passage emphasizes that the defeat of the enemy is permanent. Never again will the fortified city be rebuilt; it will disappear. Further, when the nations of the world see God's triumph, they too will be brought to worship him as the Lord. From his actions, all peoples will know who is God, especially since he will be shown to be the one sure defense of all those in need or who have no strength of their own — a thought most tellingly set forth in the Suffering Servant Song in Isaiah 52:13-15. God shows his lordship by exalting the defenseless and putting down the mighty, and of course the New Testament emphasizes that in everything from the Magnificat to the cross and resurrection. In contrast to the futile defenses of the strong and ruthless, God's might is the one sure protection.

After God has defeated his enemies, verses 6-9a go on to tell of God's banquet on Mount Sinai. And here a universal note is sounded. Not only will Israel be exalted, but God will make a luxurious feast for all peoples. His love in his kingdom will extend to all. (Another writer excludes Moab, vv. 10-12.) Best of all, God will do away with the veil of mourning and death that has laid for all centuries over humankind. Tenderly, the Lord will wipe away tears from faces and take away all reproach of his people. Then there will be the universal rejoicing and confession found in verse 9a. We have waited for the Lord, and he has saved us.

In its entirety, our text portrays for us the hope found in the Christian faith. God will bring an end to humankind's violent and sin-pocked history and will establish his good reign over all the earth. Every knee will bow to him and every tongue will confess his lordship. And in the words of the Bible's final book, "God himself will be with (us); he will wipe away every tear from (our) eyes, and death shall be no more, neither shall there be mourning nor crying nor pain any more, for the former things (will) have passed away" (Revelation 21:3-4). For that festive and joyful end we wait in certain hope. Therefore, we need never despair and we need never be crushed, no matter what our situation. Nor need we ever wonder what the world is coming to. It is coming to God. Of that joyful reign of his over all his creation, we can be very sure.

Proper 24

Exodus 33:12-23

There is no doubt, according to the stories that we find in Exodus, that the unfaithfulness of Israel in substituting worship of the golden calf for worship of the Lord caused a deep rift between God and his chosen people. Up to this time God had always accompanied his people personally in their trek through the wilderness. But God had experienced the fickleness of his people. As a result, the Lord introduces several means of mediating between himself and Israel. "I will not go up among you, lest I consume you in the way, for you are a stiff-necked people" (Exodus 33:3). Instead, God sends his angel to accompany the people (33:2). He establishes the tent of meeting outside the camp, where he can speak with Moses (33:7-11). And he sends a representative of himself (v. 14). That latter is the concern of our text for the morning.

Moses knows that he and his compatriots need God. "If thy presence will not go with me, do not carry us up from here" (v. 15). Perhaps that is the prayer of every one of us — to beg God's presence with us in every accustomed or new undertaking; for if God be against us, who can be for us? God rules this world and guides our separate and corporate lives. And if he will not go with us, we have no chance of lasting good. We are far too feeble, far too blinded by our own selfishness, far too influenced by the corrupted ways of the society around us to choose the proper paths. God must lead, or our way will end in destruction. Moses knows that, as we know it deep in our souls.

The Lord in his mercy does not desert Moses and his people. "My presence will go with you, and I will give you rest." God will guide the people to the promised land, which is always described as Israel's "place of rest" in the Old Testament. But the word for "presence" in this passage is *panim* in the Hebrew, and it means "face." It will be a hypostasis, a representative of the Lord, but it

227

will not be his full person. God will be with Israel, but only through the presence of that mediator, because Israel's sinfulness could not survive before the pure and awesome presence of God in all his glory.

Is that not the case with us also? That there must be a mediator between God and us sinners, lest we be destroyed by the unstained glory of God himself? How could you or I, with all our faults and so very human weaknesses, stand before the God of majesty who hates sin? We cannot, can we? But God does not desert us, despite our sin and indifference and disobedience toward him. Instead he gives us a mediator named Jesus Christ, who is pure, untarnished, obedient love, and Christ represents us to God and represents God in his fullness to us — not partially but God as he truly is. So every prayer we make is through the mediation or in the name of Jesus Christ. Otherwise we sinners literally do not have a prayer.

The Lord establishes means of mediation of his presence for Israel and thus continues to guide them on their way toward the promised land. And that continuing guidance is what sets Israel apart from every other nation. Israel is a "visited people," visited and guided and protected by God. "Is it not in thy going with us ... that we are distinct, I and thy people, from all other people that are upon the face of the earth?" (v. 16). The Lord God goes with her. Note that the verb is not "is" but "goes." Israel is on a journey. And so are we. Like Israel, the Christian Church is God's holy people, set apart for his purpose and accompanied by him. And it is in that "going with us" by the Lord, by means of his Spirit poured out upon us from the Father and Son, that we too are different from every other people (Romans 8; 1 Corinthians 2-3, et al.).

Moses is assured that God's "presence" will continue to go with them. But perhaps it is a mark of Moses' intimate relation with the Lord that Moses asks to see God in all his glory. Moses hungers to know God fully, as so many saints have hungered to have a "beatific vision" of the Lord. Human beings cannot see God and live (v. 20), however for every human being including Moses is stained by sin. There follows, therefore, the fascinating story in verses 21-23. God will hide Moses in a cleft in the rock and pass by him. But as God passes, he will put his hand over Moses in the cleft, and Moses will glimpse only God's back and not his face. Is that nonsensical anthropomorphism? No, we must reply that the very same God was incarnated in human flesh, and we have seen the glory of God, full of grace and truth, in the face of Jesus Christ (2 Corinthians 4:6). "We have beheld his glory, glory as of the only Son from the Father" (John 1:14).

Lutheran Option: Isaiah 45:1-7

Up until 550 B.C., the people of Judah were captives in exile to the Babylonian Empire. Then there arose Cyrus II of Persia, who captured Media, Lydia, and finally Babylonia in 539 B.C. Exercising a policy of tolerance and understanding toward captive peoples, Cyrus allowed all of the Judean exiles who wished to do so to return to Palestine and to rebuild their temple, even furnishing the funds for the reconstruction (2 Chronicles 36:22—Ezra 1:4). This text is the Lord's address to Cyrus by the mouth of the prophet Second Isaiah.

We often ignorantly believe that international affairs are in the hands of the politicians and military and multinational corporations. This text wants us to learn otherwise. Its predominant emphasis is on the work of the Lord, and everything that Cyrus accomplishes is really the action of God. Thus, all of the verbs are in the first person, with God speaking: "I have grasped," "I will go," "I will break," "I will give," "I call you," "I surname you," "I gird you." Cyrus is raised up and given his military victories by God (cf. 41:2-3, 25; 46:11; 48:14-15). God rules the world of nations, a fact that we need to remember as we contemplate our international scene.

Despite the fact that Cyrus' power and conquests come from the Lord, Cyrus does not know the Lord (vv. 4-5). God works unseen behind the actions of the Persian king. But God's work serves as a witness to all people, including Cyrus himself. God's exercise of his might through the armies of Cyrus is the sign that God is the Lord "and there is no other" (v. 6). Three times that proclamation rings out, "I am the Lord" (vv. 5, 6, 7). No human power can stand before him. God rules, and is the only God.

The biblical witness to God has two emphases, however. One is on the irresistible might of the Lord, before whom all human beings are as nothing (cf. 40:15-17). The other is on the love of God. Why has the Lord raised up Cyrus to defeat the Babylonians and to release the exiles? "For the sake of my servant Jacob, and Israel my chosen" (v. 4). God is still working out his purpose of saving his world, and he uses Cyrus as the instrument to free Israel, that she may continue to be the Lord's people, set apart for his purpose. God loves all humankind and wishes to save us all. And so he releases Israel to continue the history of salvation. God loves, but he also has the power to make his love effective, and neither one of those biblical emphases must ever be forgotten.

Indeed, God not only has power over all nations, but he also has power over all creation. He forms the light and creates the darkness (v. 7). And then follows a statement that has disturbed many people. "I make weal and create woe," God declares. Does God create woe? Does he make the suffering and trouble that we human beings experience?

We must not separate that saying from its context. Yes, God makes a lot of trouble — for the Egyptians at the time of the exodus, for the Babylonians who have exiled Judah, for Adolf Hitler and every modern tyrant, for every human being who would deter God from his good purpose of saving his creation. God makes lots of woe for those who oppose him, though we must not believe that all suffering and trouble come from the hand of God. Much of it comes from our own blindness and sinfulness. But God does put down his enemies, and he will continue to do so until he brings his salvation to all his world. We can rejoice that such a fact is true, and that God's is finally the kingdom and the power and the glory forever.

Proper 25

Deuteronomy 34:1-12

In the scriptures, the first five books of the Old Testament, or the Pentateuch, are sometimes called "The Law of Moses" (e.g. Luke 2:22; 24:44), and the book of Deuteronomy has the traditional title of "The Fifth Book of Moses." Fundamentalists therefore often hold that Moses is the author of Deuteronomy. But as has often been pointed out, if that were so, Moses would be said to have written the account of his own death. We know, further, that the list of the tribal boundaries in this text are later than the time of Moses. Therefore, while many of the Old Testament's laws come from Moses, scholars generally agree that the core of Deuteronomy dates from the seventh century B.C., while this chapter is from the hand of the Deuteronomic editors of about 550 B.C. We have no reason to doubt, however, that Moses was forbidden to enter the promised land, that the site of his grave is unknown, and that Joshua was his successor.

Moses has led his people out of Egypt, borne with them through their complaints in the wilderness, represented them in the establishment of the covenant relationship with the Lord at Mount Sinai, delivered the Ten Commandments and the Covenant Law to them from God, and traveled with them as far as the land of Moab on the eastern side of the Jordan opposite Jericho. In addition, he has delivered the three long sermons that we find in Deuteronomy, presenting the final pre-exilic form of the torah to his people and entering into a covenant renewal ceremony with them.

Now the elderly lawgiver is commanded by God to ascend Mount Nebo in the Abarim range in Moab (Deuteronomy 42:48-49). He does so and then crosses a mountain saddle to climb up to the tip of Mount Pisgah, from where the Lord shows him the promised land laid out before him. Moses sees it all, from the territory in the north where Dan will reside to the southern regions that will

231

be Judah's home, and then beyond, even to the desert of the Negev and the southern tip of the Dead Sea. Finally the homeland toward which Moses and his people have struggled for so many years is in sight. But Moses is not allowed to enter into it. Why?

There are two reasons given in the Old Testament, although one of them is obscure. Both Numbers 20:10-13 and Deuteronomy 32:51 say it is because Moses "broke faith" with God at Meribah and did not revere God in the eyes of the people. There have been numerous attempts to explain what that means on the basis of the stories in Exodus 17 and Numbers 20, but the explanation remains unclear.

The other reason, however, is not a puzzle. Moses takes the sins of the people upon himself and dies outside of the promised land in order that Israel may enter into it (Deuteronomy 1:37; 3:26; 4:21). Repeatedly, the people have not trusted the Lord and repeatedly his anger has risen against them for their faithlessness. But also repeatedly, Moses has interceded with God for his sinful people, asking that God forgive them. As we heard two Sundays ago, Moses has been the intercessor before the Lord for his faithless folk, fulfilling the function of a true prophet. But because prophets are intercessors on account of sin, they are suffering intercessors, bearing in themselves instead the punishment that God would otherwise bring upon his covenant people (cf. Hosea's marriage to a harlot, or the command to Jeremiah not to marry or to attend a party or a funeral, or the commands to Ezekiel to eat unclean and rationed food and water, or the Sufferings Servant's abuse and death — all are substitutions for what God would have done to sinful Israel). So it is too in the New Testament that the One who fulfills all the prophets bears our sins on his cross and dies the death that we should have died, in order that we may have life.

Our text makes a point of saying that no one knows where Moses is buried. The Israelites are thereby prevented from making pilgrimages to Moses' grave, from worshiping the dead, and from giving their loyalty and adoration to anyone but the Lord. God is not the God of the dead, but of the living, and all are to live to him (Luke 20:38).

232

The spirit of wisdom to lead was passed on to Joshua when Moses laid his hands on him (Deuteronomy 34:9). Joshua can successfully lead the people into the promised land only by the power of God's Spirit that was first given to Moses. Human abilities will not suffice. This is God's enterprise, and not man's (cf. Joshua 1:1-9).

Moses was a towering figure in Israel, and because he was the prophetic mediator of the Word of God and the suffering intercessor for Israel's sins, for centuries after, Israel expected that the new age of the kingdom would be ushered in by the appearance of a new "prophet like Moses" (Deuteronomy 18:15). Repeatedly, the New Testament reflects that expectation (John 1:21, 15; 6:14; 7:40), but it was not until Jesus of Nazareth appeared that Peter and Stephen could preach that the new age had broken into history and that the new Moses who suffered for the sins of the world was Jesus Christ, who was not only the expected prophet, but also God's Messiah and Son.

Lutheran Option: Leviticus 19:1-2, 15-18

Among the commandments that Moses gave to the people of Israel while they were in the wilderness, we find Leviticus 19:11-18 which is known as the Levitical Dodecalogue and which is part of the Holiness Code of Leviticus 17-26. Leviticus 19:1-18 form the priestly version of the Ten Commandments, and concern the subjects contained in that Decalogue.

The aim of this material is to make Israel a holy people, as God is holy (v. 2), and the passage gives numerous examples of the holy manner of life. Verses 3-8 concern holiness in relation to God. Verses 9-18 deal with holiness in human relationships. It is from verse 18 that Jesus takes the second great commandment, to love our neighbor as ourselves (Mark 12:31 and parallels), which Paul sees as the summary of the law (Romans 13:9; Galatians 5:14; cf. James 2:8).

We have repeatedly said that to be God's holy people means to be set apart for his purpose. But how are we to live in that separateness? What are the covenant people and we, as new persons in

233

Jesus Christ, supposed to do? This text gives very concrete illustrations, and the preacher can use any one or several of them to deal with the congregation's daily living. These are very practical commandments and obviously they can be followed. But two emphases assert themselves.

First, the holy life is one of growth in sanctification, in holiness, in goodness. No one of us is good all the time, and indeed, goodness no longer seems to be a goal in our society. We want to be rich, slim, beautiful, admired, accomplished, fun, talented. But good? How many of you sincerely want to be good? How many of you want to grow daily in goodness? That's kind of out of fashion in our society, isn't it? But we are not slaves to the ways of our society; we are slaves of Jesus Christ, as Paul says (Romans 6:16-18). And part of our discipleship for Christ is growth in goodness. Well, Leviticus here gives us some ways to grow.

These commands are laid upon us, in the second place, not as rules of human society or as mere suggestions for our conduct or as tips on how to make friends and influence people. These are commands of the Lord our God, teachings about how to have his abundant life, directions about how to walk in our daily paths according to his will and not our own. "I am the Lord your God" occurs eight times in Leviticus 19:1-18, emphasizing over and over that these commandments concern the will of God. We sometimes ask, "How do we know what God's will is?" Here is part of the answer. Here are concrete descriptions of what God wants and does not want us to do. And because we love God, and because he has given his Son that we may have eternal life, we strive for holiness, and in overwhelming gratitude, we obey this merciful guidance of our Lord.

Reformation Sunday

Joshua 3:7-17

Israel has been encamped at Shittim in the territory of Moab on the Eastern side of the Jordan River opposite Jericho. Now they prepare to cross over the river and to enter into the promised land, in fulfillment of God's promise to them. Moses has died and Joshua is now the leader.

The stories that we have in Joshua 3-5 somewhat parallel the accounts that we had of Moses, with the miraculous crossing of the water, the circumcision of the people, and the celebration of the passover. Joshua 5:4-7 tells why the repetition of the events is necessary. The first generation of Israelites that came out of Egypt, with the exception of Joshua and Caleb, died in the wilderness because of their sin against the Lord. Now their children, in the second generation, must experience the mighty acts of God as the basis of their faith.

The biblical faith must be handed down from generation to generation. Earlier in the Bible, Deuteronomy emphasizes the necessity of teaching our children what God has done. In Joshua, those children, now grown, must experience God's deeds for themselves, and so it always is. We must teach our children about the life and death and resurrection of Jesus Christ. But the marvelous fact is that when we tell about Christ and worship him, the story of our Lord remains not only a past event for our offspring, but becomes present reality for them. They experience for themselves the forgiveness, the new life, and the certain hope of the resurrection given in Christ. They can therefore live, not only on the basis of their parents' faith, but on the basis of their own experience of the facts of that faith.

In our text, the ark of the covenant once again becomes important in the story. Exodus 25:10-22 detailed the construction of the ark on Mount Sinai and is the only description we have of it. It was a rectangular box about 50 x 30 x 30 inches in size, overlaid in gold. It had rings on its corners with poles through the rings, so the ark could be carried. On top was a slab of gold called the "mercy seat," and at each end of the mercy seat, facing one another, was a cherub with outspread wings. Most important, however, the ark was considered to be the base of the throne of the Lord, who was enthroned invisibly above it (1 Samuel 4:4). Therefore, where the ark was, the Lord was present, and there Moses could meet with God to receive his commandments for the people (Exodus 25:22). When in our text Joshua commands the priests to carry the ark into the ford of the Jordan, the thought is that God is entering the water ahead of the people, and it is God who causes the waters to gather in a heap so the people may cross over on dry land, just as it was God who rolled back the waters of the Reed Sea at the time of the exodus. This is God's majestic working over the forces of nature. Indeed, God's command of the waters is the sign to the Israelites that their Lord is among them (v. 10).

Certainly throughout the scriptures, God's working in the natural world is a testimony to the power of God, as it should be a testimony also to us. The God who raised up the Rocky Mountains and who ignited the sun has unimaginable might. But we should note carefully: the God of the Bible is not *in* nature or identified with it. Rather, he is Lord *over* nature and can do with it what he will. And that serves as an assurance to the Israelites in our text that God has the power also to defeat the enemies whom they will meet in the promised land (v. 10). He is Lord not only of nature but also of nations.

If we did not have the biblical accounts of God's working in the history of Israel and supremely, in Jesus Christ, however, we would never correctly read the testimony to him in the world of nature. We would turn him into a nature god, as many have done, or believe him only a God of power. And we would never know him above all as a God of love. But pure, undefiled, merciful love he is, and so in our text, he leads his covenant people safely across the Jordan and into the land that he has promised them.

Lutheran Option: Jeremiah 31:31-34

Our text for this Reformation Sunday in our church year is Jeremiah's famous announcement of God's promise of a new covenant with a new, reunited Israel and Judah. The time is 588 B.C. when Jeremiah delivers this promise. Jerusalem is under siege by the armies of the Babylonian Empire. Her surrounding territory has been lost, just as the ten northern tribes were much earlier lost to Assyria. The situation within the city's walls is desperate, with rationing of food and water. Shortly the walls will be breached, the temple will be destroyed, the city ravaged, and all but the poorest peasants will be carried into Babylonian exile. All will take place as God's punishment for Judah's idolatry and injustice and forgetfulness of her covenant with her Lord. In the holocaust of exile, God will deal with Israel's sin against him.

Judgment, however, is never God's last word. Into the midst of Israel's desperate situation, God injects his word by the mouth of his prophet. There will come a time, the Lord promises, when he will restore the whole of Israel and make with her a new covenant. Israel broke the Sinai covenant, despite God's tender love toward her through all her history. But God will reestablish a new relationship with his people by writing the words of a new covenant on her heart. Once again God will be Israel's God, and she will be his people (the covenant formula), willingly following his commandments and trusting him from the depths of her heart. All will know him and obey him willingly, and all their past sin will be forgiven in the joyful new relationship with their God.

As is the case throughout the Bible, new life and communion with God involves the transformation of human hearts. Our sinfulness starts within our hearts and festers there and breaks forth in corruption of the life of neighborhoods and societies and nations. To be God's faithful people, we must be made new from the inside out, so that we freely and joyfully follow God's ways and not our own. And sadly, we cannot work that transformation by ourselves. Our wills to new life are too feeble, our satisfactions with our old life too deep, our selfishness and pride too persistent to lead us to purify our thoughts and actions. Only God can recreate us and make us good. And the promise of this text is that God will do so, not only for Israel, but for all of us.

The question then is: Did God ever keep his promise? Did he in fact make a new covenant with us sinners? Did he give us the possibility of goodness and righteousness, of love and joy and peace with him and our neighbors? The answer is an unqualified "Yes." When Jesus Christ reclined at table on the night he was betrayed, after he had given the bread symbolizing his death for our sins on his cross, he also took the cup, and when he had blessed it, he gave it to his disciples and said, "This is the new covenant in my blood. All of you, drink of it." And then he sealed that covenant with his cross and resurrection.

More than that, after his ascension to the right hand of the Father, Christ poured into our hearts his Spirit, and by that Spirit, writes Paul, all of us are being transformed into Christ's likeness (2 Corinthians 3:18), so that we can love as he loves, obey as he obeys, trust as he trusts, serve as he serves. "If anyone is in Christ, he (or she) is a new creation" (2 Corinthians 5:17). The new life of the new covenant is given us by our Lord, by his Spirit dwelling in us and making us new.

All Saints' Sunday

Revelation 7:9-17

Our text for the morning brings three burning questions about human existence into focus for us. First, is there any justice in the eternal scheme of things? That is, is there any reward for those who have lived a good and faithful life with God on this earth? Certainly those who try to live righteous, obedient, trusting lives do not thereby escape the sufferings that come upon other human beings. The good man is as likely to die of cancer as the evil man. The faithful woman can experience as many burdens and troubles as the unfaithful. And both good and bad end up in the darkness of the grave. So is there any advantage in trying to walk faithfully in the way with our God?

Second, does the evil we see in our society all around us have the last word? Will the violence, the bloodshed, the hatreds, the turmoils of human communities always persist in human life, until we finally destroy ourselves and our environment? Or is there a better destiny for the human race?

And third, what has happened to those beloved Christian friends so dear to our hearts who have died and whose passing has left us with sorrow and yearning for their kindly presence? Our text for this All Saints' Sunday gives us at least some hints of the answers.

The picture here in the book of Revelation comes to us from a vision that a Christian named John was given at the end of the first century A.D., after he had been banished to the small island of Patmos in the Aegean Sea, off the western coast of Asia Minor. John, who was a different John from the author of the fourth Gospel, wrote Revelation to encourage Christians in seven churches in Asia Minor to remain faithful to Christ, despite the fact that they faced persecution by Roman authorities under the rule of the Emperor Domitian (A.D. 81-96).

239

Our particular text envisions the throne room of Almighty God at the end of human history, and it does so in highly mysterious and sometimes bizarre language, suitable to such an unearthly vision. After all, it is very difficult to talk of heavenly things in earthly language. But present beside the throne of God is Jesus Christ, the Lamb of God, who has opened a scroll of final judgments that the Lord God is about to loose on those who have opposed his rule.

Standing before the throne are 144,000 faithful Jewish Christians, 12,000 from each of the twelve tribes of Israel, who have followed Christ (vv. 4-8). And with them is a great multitude from every nation on earth, clad in white robes, with palm branches in their hands. Elders, that is, leaders of the Jewish Christians, inquire who the white-robed persons are, to which is replied, "These are they who have come out of the great tribulation" (vv. 13-14). That is, the multitude of persons is made up of those who have been persecuted for their faith, but who have remained steadfast and faithful through all of their trials, and who now are standing before the throne of God in heaven, making up a great multitude who praise the Lord.

Well, do you wonder what has become of the faithful Christians whom you have known during your lifetime — steady souls who have never wavered in their trust in Jesus Christ? They now stand in heaven before the throne of God, this vision tells us. And they enjoy a wondrous existence. They no longer suffer any want. They hunger and thirst no more, nor suffer any bodily discomfort. They know no more sorrow. God shelters them with his presence, and Christ guides them like a shepherd, refreshing them with the waters of eternal life, and their eternal joy is to serve their God and to be with him forever (vv. 15-17).

Is there any better outcome for faithful living, good Christians, than that which this vision presents us, any greater reward, any more desired goal? All our lives as Christians, all our worship, all our service have been directed toward achieving fellowship and a daily communion with God through Jesus Christ. We have sought after that in every prayer, every Bible study, every Christian action. And here, at the end, says John, is the fulfillment — eternal life with God, who is only good and merciful and loving. Can you imagine knowing God face to face and living in the fullness of his love? That is almost incomprehensible to us, and yet, says our text, that is the wondrous outcome.

As for the evil and wrong that we see daily in our society and that we read about in every morning headline. No, says our text. They do not have the last word, for God is in fact going to bring his kingdom on earth even as it is in heaven. The kingdoms of this earth will indeed become the kingdom of our Lord and of his Christ. There is a final judgment coming, writes John, a final justice, a final balancing of the good and of the evil. And God will do away with all his enemies and forever banish Satan and all who have opposed God's lordly rule. Earth will be fair again, and God will be able to look at his whole creation and say once again, as he said at the beginning, "Behold, it is very good" (cf. Genesis 1:31).

But that brings us up short, doesn't it? Because we know that we too have not always been faithful Christians. We too have not always trusted God. We too have not followed our Lord Christ every day. Can we then expect to survive in this last terrible judgment that Revelation portrays for us?

John gives us one sentence to assure us. Those white robed martyrs in the multitude of which he writes have "washed their robes and made them white in the blood of the Lamb" (v. 14) — a familiar saying and yet somewhat bizarre for us. But what it means is that through our trust in the death and resurrection of Jesus Christ, we have been forgiven and counted righteous in the eyes of God. We are a forgiven company, good Christians, when we trust in Christ's work. We are made members of a justified multitude when we confess our sins and place our lives in the merciful hands of our Lord. And because of the love and forgiveness that God has poured out on us through his Son, we can be members of that faithful company of saints who have eternal life in the company of our God.

Surely our response to such merciful love can only be that which we find in the hymns that are recorded in our text: "Salvation belongs to our God who sits upon the throne, and to the Lamb" (v. 10). "Blessing and glory and wisdom and thanksgiving and honor and power and might be to our God for ever and ever! Amen" (v. 12).

Proper 28

Judges 4:1-7

It is somewhat of a mystery as to why this one text from Judges is inserted into the lectionary at this point. The Lutheran selection fits much better with the New Testament readings. But perhaps this is a feeble attempt to remind the congregation that women, too, served as leaders in ancient Israel.

After Israel entered into the promised land about 1220 B.C., for the next two centuries until the beginning of the reign of Saul in 1020 B.C., the people were very loosely organized as disparate and scattered tribes into a covenant federation that met together either every one or seven years at a central shrine where the ark of the covenant was located, first at Shechem, then Gilgal, and finally at Shiloh. (Even this loose organization has been questioned by some scholars.)

During this period, the Israelite tribes were constantly harassed by the surrounding Canaanites, who were more numerous and who had the military advantage of possessing horses and chariots. In our text, it is the Canaanites of the northern portion of the land around Hazor, under the kingship of one Jabin and the military leadership of Sisera, who threaten the Israelites' existence.

The Deuteronomic editors, who made the final assembly of the book of Judges, place the stories of the various Judges within a stereotyped theological framework. Israel's time in the promised land is the time of her testing, to see if she will remain faithful to her God. But, say the editors, Israel constantly falls into idolatry and worships the fertility gods and goddesses of the Canaanites. As a result, God sends his punishment upon her in the form of an attack by the surrounding Canaanites. The people cry out in repentance, according to the framework, and the Lord sends them a deliverer, a Judge, to save them from the enemy. Thus, in our text, the Lord has subjected his people to the oppression of Sisera's army.

The Judge at the time is the prophetess Deborah. She is not a military leader like many of the Judges, but rather exercises a judicial function, deciding the legal disputes that are brought to her (v. 5). Nevertheless, it is Deborah who summons Barak from the tribe of Zebulon, to lead in the battle. She commands him to call forth 10,000 of the farmers in the northern tribes of Naphtali and Zebulon to fight against the superior Canaanites. And because she is a prophetess, she can foretell that God will defeat the Canaanites (v. 7) and that the Canaanite commander will be slain by a woman (v. 9). In the following story those events take place (vv. 12-24).

The notable fact in our text, however, is that God is the one who determines the course of events. "*I* will draw out Sisera ... *I* will give him into your hand ...*" says the Lord through Deborah (v. 7). Israel is God's covenant people, and it is God who protects and delivers them, because they are the instruments of the purpose of God to bring his blessing on all the families of the earth (cf. Genesis 12:3; Exodus 19:6). Despite Israel's idolatry, despite her continual apostasy and unfaithfulness, God forgives his errant people and moves their history forward toward his goal of salvation for the world.

It is not far fetched to conclude therefore that God is still doing the same thing in our history. Heaven knows we are frequently unfaithful servants, giving our loyalty and worship to everything and everyone except our Lord. But we are also members, with Israel, of God's covenant people, who have been set aside to be God's instruments in the salvation of all peoples. And God is using us — using even our little sporadic faithfulness and service — to bring in his kingdom on earth. It is not we who live, but Christ who lives in us, and he will bring our history to his blessed conclusion.

Lutheran Option: Zephaniah 1:7, 12-18

Our text encompasses the seventh century B.C. prophet's announcement of the nearness of the Day of the Lord, of the *dies irae*, the day of wrath — the fearful day at the end of human history when God invades the earth to destroy all of those who oppose him, before he brings in his kingdom.

We live in an age and a society that believes that God never judges anybody. Too often we picture God as a kindly helper who overlooks every wrong and whose task it is simply to forgive us our sins and to deliver us out of any difficulty that we may find ourselves in. So we go our merry ways, ignoring God's loving commandments for us, making up the rules of right and wrong as we go along, and considering ourselves the individual sovereigns over our own lives and our chosen futures.

The results are the chaos in our world, of which we read in the morning headlines, and the agonizing thought that there really is no good future. No. No one rules except us. And try as we may in our decent moments, we seem unable to establish any lasting peace or community of love on our tortured earth. Millions starve, more millions die violently, our streets echo with gunfire and are besmirched with the crime that keeps us behind locked doors. Families fall apart, hatreds fester, and children find themselves bereft of caring parents or education. And we dimly realize that death will be our only deliverance from a sin-saturated life that will never finally know improvement.

But our text gives assurance of a different outcome. To be sure, it is full of darkness and gloom, distress and anguish. God has risen up in warfare against his enemies, says Zephaniah. He has offered that sacrifice that precedes every Israelite battle (cf. 1 Samuel 13:5-12). Now his final judgment is at hand, and he will come to do away with every human military weapon (cf. Isaiah 9:5; Psalm 46:8-9) and every sinful soul who has thought that human beings rule the world and that they are in charge. No material wealth, paid to government or church, will be able to turn aside God's onslaught (v. 18). God in his just judgment will destroy those who have forgotten and defied him. For he is Ruler and Lord over all, and he comes to reclaim his creation.

When the last judgment will take place, Zephaniah does not say, any more than does the New Testament (cf. Mark 13:32-37). The Day of the Lord comes like a thief in the night, reports our epistle lesson. Who knows? Maybe that dreadful day will come tomorrow afternoon! And our Lord's warning to us is to be ready and to "watch."

So our text is finally a call to repentance, isn't it? And a call to the renewal of our trust in Christ's deliverance of us. Writes Paul, "For God has not destined us for wrath, but to obtain salvation through our Lord Jesus Christ" (1 Thessalonians 5:9).

What will the outcome be, then? Zephaniah tells us of it. "For I will leave in the midst of you a people humble and lowly. They shall seek refuge in the name of the Lord, those who are left in Israel. They shall do no wrong and utter no lies, nor shall there be found in their mouth a deceitful tongue. For they shall pasture and lie down, and none shall make them afraid" (Zephaniah 3:12-13).

Truly I say to you, "The Kingdom of God will come."

Christ the King

Ezekiel 34:11-16, 20-24

The temptation of the preacher in using these passages from Ezekiel is to lapse into a sentimental discussion of the gentleness and love of Christ, the good Shepherd. We must remember, however, that the term "shepherd" in the Bible and the ancient Near East, most often refers not to a kindly herdsman, but to a king or to a leader of the people. These texts are therefore eminently appropriate to the Sunday celebrating the kingship of our Lord.

In his first 24 chapters, the prophet Ezekiel pronounces God's stern judgment on the sinfulness of Judah, a judgment that leads to its final destruction by the armies of the Babylonian Empire in 587 B.C. Chapters 25-32 contain oracles against the foreign nations. Chapter 33 announces the fall of Jerusalem to the armies of Nebuchadnezzar II in 598 B.C. In March of 597 B.C., the davidic King Jehoichin was deported to Babylonia, along with the upper classes and leaders of the Judean community, including the prophet Ezekiel. The temple and royal treasures were drained, and the puppet Zedekiah was installed on the Judean throne. Our prophet therefore speaks from his situation in Babylonian exile, after his call to be a prophet in 593 B.C., and beginning in chapter 34, he proclaims God's future restoration of his people.

If we look at the context of Ezekiel 34:11-16, it is clear that the prophet holds King Jehoiakim and the leaders of Judah largely responsible for the sins of the people (vv. 1-10). "... the shepherds have fed themselves and have not fed my sheep" (v. 8). The weak and poor have not been protected, the hurting have not been comforted and healed. Injustice and idolatry have been rife, with the king and leaders seeking only their own selfish interests (cf. Jeremiah's similar indictment in Jeremiah 22). As the king and leaders have done, so the people have done — a piercing judgment that could easily apply to our own time in the United States.

The leaders of a people set the moral and physical direction and tone of a populace, and as a result, the people have suffered.

The Lord God, however, is in charge, not only of the lives of individuals, but also of the affairs of nations. And so to his compatriots in exile, Ezekiel announces that the time will come when God himself will be the King, Protector, and Savior of the exiled Judeans, as in reality he has always been King. God will seek out all of those scattered in exile and restore them to a good and abundant life in the land of Israel. He will find the lost, and minister to the hurting, and strengthen the weak (v. 16). But significantly, he will also keep an eye on the strong, so that they do not use their power and strength once more to oppress their subjects. God will establish justice in the land, and no one will be in want.

God's monitoring of any powerful leaders of his flock is further dealt with in verses 17-24. But apparently verses 17-19 deal with leaders of the exiled community. There have been dissension and injustices among the exiles, as we know from Jeremiah 29. And some of the exiles have not repented nor do they believe Ezekiel's proclamations (cf. Ezekiel 33:30-33). Therefore God will deal with those oppressors and dissenters too (vv. 20-21). But the prophet does not say what their fate will be.

Instead, God will set over all of his people a new davidic king to rule and guide their life (v. 22). The new David will be "prince" over the people, that is, he will be given his rule by God and established in it as God's representative. Further, he will be their one Shepherd, and the people will be one people, with no divisions among them. No other authority will rule their life. From the new David will come the people's sustenance and direction for all their living. The people will be faithful, for God will be their God (the first half of the covenant formula), with no other idol or deity claiming their ultimate loyalty. And none shall make them a prey.

The surety of this promise is affirmed, then, in the last phrase of verse 24: "I, the Lord, have spoken." The Word of the Lord will stand forever (cf. Isaiah 40:8). God will never take back his Word or ever let it go unfulfilled. He will keep his spoken promise and bring it to fruition.

This promise of God's, delivered by the prophet Ezekiel, is

one of the many promises that the prophets include in their preaching about the coming from God of a new davidic king. The prophets proclaim that promise through four centuries of their preaching (cf. Isaiah 11:1-9; 32:1; Jeremiah 23:5-6; Hosea 3:5; Amos 9:11-12; Micah 5:2-4; Zechariah 6:9-14; 9:9-10; 12:8). And the promise is entirely consistent with God's original promise to David that there will never be lacking a davidic heir to sit upon the throne (2 Samuel 7:16). In Ezekiel's time, the line of David has been interrupted by the exile of the davidic Jehoiachin, of whose end we are not told (cf. 2 Kings 25:27-30). Nor does Ezekiel know how God will continue the davidic line. But what he is given to know is that a new David will come to rule over the covenant people, and it is that Word, put in his mouth by God, that he faithfully proclaims.

It is no accident, therefore, that the New Testament begins with the phrase, "Jesus Christ, the son of David...." Throughout its stories it tells us that Jesus Christ is born in the city of David, as a descendant of that great king, that he is hailed by the crowds as he rides into Jerusalem on a donkey, on what we call Palm Sunday, as the "Son of David" (Matthew 21:9), and that even Pontius Pilate has to confess, according to the Fourth Gospel, that Christ is "King of the Jews" (John 18:33—19:22). God has kept all of those promises given us through the centuries by the prophets, and Jesus comes to us this Sunday as God's representative, God's Prince, God's only begotten Son, God's King.

We should note, however, that he is the King who *rules* over our life, and from whom we are to find our sustenance and our sole guidance. He gives and supplies our life, the New Testament tells us, and he guides our lives, not only through all of his commandments in the scriptures but also through his Holy Spirit, shed upon us through biblical reading and preaching and sacrament. It is by his Word and his Spirit that we are to live our Christians lives and by no other.

We should also note that in our text for the morning it is stressed that the new davidic king will establish justice in the land. Christ's rule is not only merciful, it is also firm and just. And so our King expects us to establish justice in our society — to protect the weak, to help the poor, to succor the hurting, to keep the powerful from abusing their power. We have a long way to go before we realize those expectations in our country and in our world. But those acts are commanded us by our King, and if we love him and serve him, we will obey his commandments. Yes, Christ is our King. Let us render to him the worship and obedience that his kingship deserves.

Thanksgiving Day

Deuteronomy 8:7-18

Our text for this day is about forgetting and remembering. Indeed, the whole eighth chapter of Deuteronomy concerns those two thoughts. Repeating the words, the chapter says, "And you shall remember ..." (v. 2); "Take heed lest you forget ..." (v. 11); "Then your heart be lifted up and you forget ..." (v. 14); "You shall remember ..." (v. 18); "And if you forget" (v. 19).

It is a pertinent emphasis for us, for we live in an age and a society that has forgotten. We have forgotten the Lord our God. Many of us share our society's notion these days that we are separate, free, autonomous, self-fulfilling individuals, whose lives and future are entirely in our own hands. If we accomplish something, our own talents and brains have been our instruments. If we fail, we haven't kept our eye on the ball or we've just been unlucky or the victim of unforeseen circumstances. Our days are in our own hands, and it is up to us to make something of them. Thus our society is largely a secular society, and you and I are frequently secularists, that is, we believe we are living our lives apart from the presence and working of God. God has little hand in what we do or in what happens to us. God is absent and forgotten.

We are therefore very much like the Israelites in our text. They have fled their slavery in Egypt and trekked through a dry and dusty wilderness filled with snakes and scorpions and burning heat. But finally their second generation has reached the eastern bank of the Jordan River, and they are now looking over into the land of Palestine. Before they cross the Jordan River, however, their leader Moses addresses them in the three long sermons we find in Deuteronomy. Our text forms a part of the first sermon. And what is Moses' emphasis? "Remember the Lord your God" (v. 18). "... remember all the way which the Lord your God has led you" (v. 2).

251

The Lord led Israel for over forty years after her release from Egyptian slavery. He brought her out of the house of bondage and guided her through the wilderness by pillar by day and fire by night. He quenched her thirst with water from a rock and gave her daily bread from the manna. He even prevented her clothing from wearing out, says Deuteronomy, and her weary feet from swelling (v. 4). And all of that was simply grace on the Lord's part, gracious actions toward his chosen people whom he loved for no reason at all. They complained all through the forty years, as we so often complain. They attempted to follow their own path and were subjected to a humiliating defeat at Hormah (Numbers 14:39-45), as so often our self-guided stubbornness leads us too into some misery. But despite their rebellion and stubbornness and repeated sin against him, God brought his beloved people to the edge of the land he had promised them.

That's our story, too, is it not? That God has led us through all our years and brought us to the threshold of his eternal kingdom? We too were once enslaved — enslaved to sin and death — and God delivered us from our slavery through the cross and resurrection of Jesus Christ. We too have wandered our own wildernesses and suffered wants and fears. But God has preserved our lives and given us comfort and strength. We too have thirsted and hungered for healing, for love, for forgiveness, and God has poured those out upon us through the mercy of his Son.

But as we read our text, we also find that Moses proclaims a promise for Israel's future. "The Lord your God is bringing you into a good land, a land of brooks of waters, of fountains and springs ... wheat and barley ... vines and fig trees and pomegranates ... olive trees and honey ... a land in which you shall lack nothing" (vv. 7-9). And that too could be a description of our life, could it not? That we live in a land where most of us actually lack no necessity. Oh sure, we wish we had a higher salary, or could afford a new carpet for the living room. We wonder how we're going to pay college tuition or save enough for retirement. But lack, genuine lack? No, we'll manage, and none of us is truly wanting.

Moses' following words pierce to the heart of the matter, however. "Beware lest you say in your heart, 'My power and the might

252

of my hand have gotten me this wealth' " (v. 17). No. "You shall remember the Lord your God" (v. 18).

So what is Thanksgiving, good Christians? It is not the secularism of the society around us, but rather is it not that remembering? Remembering all the way that God has led us through our lives? Like Israel, we have often rebelled against our Lord and stubbornly followed our own ways. Like Israel, we have not deserved God's love that will not let us go. And now on this day of gratitude, we are asked to remember. We are bidden to call to mind the fact that we are never on our own — alone, self-fulfilled, isolated from the working of the Lord. Rather, we are constantly seen by his eyes and continually held by his hand, and sustained and guided, forgiven and loved through all our nights and days. Will we remember that, not only on this one special day, but through all our days to come? Remember and do not forget, our father Moses says to us.

Surely in a secular society such as ours we need help in remembering God, however. And that is one of the functions of the regular worship of the church. When we come to this sanctuary every Sunday morning, we are acknowledging that we do not live by our own powers, but that there is One who works and lives in us far beyond our abilities and strengths. We remember that God leads our lives, and so we come here to praise him and thank him for his love — for all the way he has led us in the past and for all his gifts and presence in the future with us.

But beyond our weekly practice of worship, we also remember God when we pray. Indeed, regular, daily, consistent prayer is an exercise in remembrance, in acknowledging the fact that there is always a Lord God beyond us. So we pray him little "arrow prayers" — one sentence words of thanks for giving us our families or for bringing us through some trouble, praise for his gift of sunlight and beauty on a glorious morn, gratitude for a night of rest and for keeping us safe for another day, words of petition for someone who is ill or for comfort in our suffering. But beyond the little sentence prayers, we also set aside a time each day for prayer. And we meditate on the Lord and remember all that he has done for us.

If we pray regularly, good Christians, we cannot forget God. And we do that because we know God has never forgotten us.

Remember and do not forget the Lord your God. Like Israel in our text, you and I stand on the eastern side of this life, gazing over into the promised land. Our land of promise is not Palestine, however, but eternal life, filled with abundance and joy beyond all our imagining. So remember God and trust him, for he will indeed lead us, as he always led Israel, into that blessed promised place of his everlasting kingdom.

Index of Biblical Texts
in Canonical Order